BEFORE BIG BLUE

BEFORE
BIG BLUE

SPORTS AT THE
UNIVERSITY OF KENTUCKY
1880-1940

Gregory Kent Stanley

THE UNIVERSITY PRESS OF KENTUCKY

Permission is gratefully acknowledged to reprint materials that originally appeared in the following forms: " 'Not Conducive to the Best Interests of This Institution': President James Kennedy Patterson, the Board of Trustees, and University of Kentucky Athletics, 1890-1910," *Filson Club History Quarterly* (April 1995); and " ' . . . And Not to Make Athletes of Them': Banning Women's Sports at the University of Kentucky," *Register of the Kentucky Historical Society* (Autumn 1995).

All photographs courtesy of the University of Kentucky Archives.

Editorial and Sales Offices: The University Press of Kentucky
663 South Limestone Street, Lexington, Kentucky 40508-4008

96 97 98 99 00   5 4 3 2 1

Library of Congress Cataloging-in-Publication Data

Stanley, Gregory Kent, 1958–
    Before Big Blue : sports at the University of Kentucky, 1880–1940
    / Gregory Kent Stanley.
        p.   cm.
    Includes bibliographical references and index.
    ISBN 0–8131–1991–X (cloth : alk. paper)
    1. University of Kentucky—Sports—History.   I. Title.
GV691.U544S83   1996
796'.0976947—dc20   96–10878

This book is printed on acid-free recycled paper meeting
the requirements of the American National Standard
for Permanence of Paper for Printed Library Materials.

Manufactured in the United States of America

CONTENTS

□

ILLUSTRATIONS

□

TABLES

PREFACE

OVER THE COURSE of the period studied here (from 1880 to 1940), terminology, especially college names, changed frequently. For example, Transylvania University adopted that name in the early nineteenth century. By late century, it was known as Kentucky University before reverting back to Transylvania. The University of Kentucky began as its Agricultural and Mechanical extension. When it separated in 1878, it was known by a succession of titles, including Kentucky State College, Kentucky State University, and finally the University of Kentucky. Except in notes, the modern titles are used throughout.

Similar title confusion surrounds Centre College. At the turn of the century, Central University of Richmond (later renamed Eastern Kentucky University) merged briefly with Centre College of Danville, prompting an interesting lawsuit over endowments. During this time the name Central University applied to the merged institutions.[1] To eliminate confusion, Centre will be used to refer to the Danville college. Central will be used only to refer to the Richmond school.

Readers interested in examining the notes in this work should be aware of the irregular pagination of the Lexington Herald. When the paper adopted a separate section for sports, business, and occasionally other topics, it did not employ a uniform method of numbering its pages. Sometimes the edition was numbered sequentially throughout. Often (but not always), especially in weekend editions, a second section began with the page number one with no reference to a new section (such as B-1). Therefore, a story that a note indicates can be found on page one may be found in an interior section of the paper.

The reader should also note the bias of the *Herald*. Not only was it of a Democratic political slant (as opposed to its Republican counterpart, the *Leader*), but it had a broader streak of yellow journalism running through it. It could be counted on to cover gruesome accidents, lynchings, or executions anywhere in the nation. Whether because of this or not, the *Herald* gave sports more extensive coverage than did the *Leader*. The paper also had a strong pro-Transylvania bias. Its articles often went to great lengths to stir up support for Transylvania's athletic program, even in the days of that program's decline.

James Kennedy Patterson, president of UK, believed that the paper conspired to tarnish the image of the university by the sensational coverage of unflattering campus incidents. The students, it appeared, concurred and on one occasion chased a *Herald* reporter from the college grounds with a barrage of stones. Patterson, a fierce disciplinarian, did not even attempt to reprimand these students, claiming that the reporter, Denny B. Goode, had not really been hurt and that the students had sufficient provocation for their disorderly conduct. The UK board of trustees and faculty debated this matter briefly. Their views were summed up by longtime professor of Greek and Latin (and university vice-president), John Neville, who earnestly hoped that in the future, the college would be spared further visitations from *Herald* reporters, "whether they be Goode, bad, or indifferent."[2]

One comment concerning Patterson is in order at the outset. Students of Kentucky history may well know that Patterson was nearly always photographed with a crutch. A childhood accident (at the age of four) crippled him for life. Accordingly, he never participated in athletics. But his objections to college sports rested upon a much deeper philosophical foundation. Patterson was a deep and complex person of great kindness, wisdom, and many well-publicized idiosyncrasies. It was not, as some have suggested, his lameness but rather his beliefs about the proper training and discipline for his students that prompted him to lash out against the university athletic program.[3]

A final note of clarification: the various city and campus newspapers often did not employ precise terminology in referring to the sports leagues to which the university belonged over the years. After UK pulled out of the Kentucky Intercollegiate Athletic Association, it joined the Southern Intercollegiate Athletic Association. That organization added so many teams (one *Herald* article listed thirty-three member institutions) that it became unwieldy. The greatest difficulty stemmed from the diverse membership in the conference. The league responded by applying different rules to different colleges depending upon their size. Unhappy with this arrangement, fifteen of the largest members left and formed the Southern Intercollegiate Conference, which also grew over the years. In 1932, it split, forming what are today the Southeastern Conference and the Atlantic Coast Conference. The *Herald*, as well as student publications such as the *Kernel* (newspaper) and the *Kentuckian* (yearbook), often used the term "Southern Conference" as an all-encompassing label. This is unfortunate because the Southern Intercollegiate Athletic Conference, Southern Conference, and the Southeastern Conference were all separate entities.[4]

During the many years that I worked on this project, I had the good fortune to receive assistance from several people. It is a pleasure to try to thank them now. Without the able assistance of Bill Marshall, Pam Brackett, and Frank Stanger of the University of Kentucky archives, this work would have been impossible. Thanks also go to Mark Summers of UK's history department and Bob Brigham at Vassar College for their patient advice and encouragement. Richard Hamm of the State University of New York not only read drafts of the manuscript but was also instrumental in opening many professional doors that appeared to be closed. I cannot thank my wife, Judy Cornett, enough for her assistance, advice, patience, and support. My Lexington friends, Charles Walsh and Rees Day, opened their homes to me during the many research trips undertaken after I had moved from the Bluegrass to Georgia. Ruby Hardin of the UK Alumni Association also arranged living quarters for me.
Nearly twenty years ago, Jim Stanley (a former Letcher County

high school sports star) gave me an athletic scholarship to attend Oklahoma State University. In doing so he not only assured that his big brother's son could attend college but he also gave me a very in-depth look at big-time college athletics that has shaped my perspective on the issue of collegiate sports. This work is dedicated to my father, Charles E. Stanley, the finest Kentuckian of all.

INTRODUCTION

COLLEGE SPORTS PROGRAMS OCCUPY a prominent place in American culture today. They are often the single most visible element of a particular institution of higher learning, revered and reviled, it seems, simultaneously. Fans follow the exploits of their favorite team with a religious fervor. At the same time, critics condemn sports for degrading the true mission of higher education. Yet, those who complain of the present situation cannot hail the past as "the good old days" of pure athletics. Any examination of the past reveals that the sins of collegiate sports today are in actuality quite old. Recruiting scandals, poor classroom performance and low graduation rates of athletes, payments to players, and the perception that the salaries of coaches are too high in relation to faculty pay all date back nearly a century in the history of college sports.

Few sports programs in the nation can match the success of the University of Kentucky. The university's facilities are among the finest anywhere, and the devotion of its fans is the stuff of legend. Unfortunately, so too have been the school's athletic scandals. Numerous university presidents have complained that these scandals tarnished the image of the entire school. During the university's early years, sports programs often found their position with the administration to be precarious. In fact UK's first president, James Kennedy Patterson, attempted to ban all sports, believing that their legacy was limited to broken noses, legs, and arms, wasted time, idleness, and "a heritage of demoralization."[1]

A study of athletics at the university reveals far more than merely the history of sports. It gives clear insights into the structure of power at the school. Patterson led several campaigns to eradicate sports. Indeed, on two occasions he succeeded in banning football. Moreover, once during his tenure, the school banned basketball. These prohibitions were only temporary. Without fail, the programs came back. Both Patterson and Frank McVey (president from 1917 to 1940) tried to assert greater control but were thwarted by the athletic support among the trustees and alumni. Presidents at other universities experienced a similar lack of success in curbing sports programs that they disliked. Some university administrations banned sports, most notably football, several times, only to see them return. The president alone did not have enough power to eliminate programs so popular among alumni and students. The faculty, on the other hand, did not have the time to supervise the athletic program. Especially in the early years, the faculty lacked the knowledge or the interest to serve as a regulatory body. As a result, many colleges formed faculty committees to supervise the sports programs.[2] At UK (especially after the retirement of Patterson), this arrangement meant that only those faculty members who were keenly interested in sports had a voice in their supervision. Patterson's successor, Henry Barker, was an avid sports fan and placed the management of sports in the hands of an athletic director and a committee stacked with sympathetic faculty members. This body answered only to the university president, effectively insulating the athletic program from critical scrutiny.

For many decades, therefore, athletics operated with only the slightest control of the university administration. It was not until the athletic department found itself deep in financial trouble in the late 1930s that McVey was able to restructure the program. He could not proceed, however, until the athletic program had lost the support of the alumni, students, and even players. The shakeup that ensued may have seemed harsh to some UK fans, but it was much milder than the sanctions levied against sports at other schools. At nearly the same time that McVey took his action, Robert Maynard Hutchins, president of the University of Chicago, decided that his program (long at the forefront of college football) could not be redeemed. Hutchins and the school's administration banned the sport in order to safeguard the true function of the university.[3]

A study of sports also reveals a great deal about the social values of the time. The question of why college sports, especially football, survived is an intriguing one. Specifically, if so many critics denounced it as brutal and corrupt and so many college presidents tried to banish it from their campuses, why did the game prove so enduring at the University of Kentucky as well as other American colleges? The game appeared on campuses at a time when many intellectuals began fearing the loss of virility because of rapid urbanization and the supposed loss of the frontier. In view of such sentiments, football served as a valuable symbol of manliness at institutions of higher learning. James R. Day, chancellor of Syracuse University, wrote that football "or any game containing elements of danger" was necessary to the development of young men.[4] The University of Kentucky student yearbook concurred, noting that football annihilated "the society dude and the cigarette worm [and] for this, if nothing else, it deserved well of the state."[5]

The nation's love of football early in this century also reveals what Americans believed to be "acceptable risks." The *Lexington Herald*, ever one for sensational reporting, described in vivid detail the many football fatalities during the early years studied here. Most notable was the *Herald's* account of the death of Naval Academy football player Earl Wilson, who broke his neck in a 1909 game. The *Herald* followed his case for months, describing in graphic detail the surgery performed to remove crushed pieces of vertebra from his spinal cord. Wilson "hovered between life and death" for six months before dying, presumably from respiratory failure.[6] In reporting the nineteen fatalities of 1910, the newspaper did not call for stricter rules or an end to the game. In fact, the *Herald* suggested that such a tally was cause for celebration and proof that new rules had eliminated much of the game's danger. The paper noted that the number of deaths the year before had been twenty-nine.

The *Herald* never called for the end of football. It never ran an editorial pleading for greater safety. Generally, it dismissed serious or fatal accidents as freak occurrences caused by inexperienced players. In describing Wilson's injury, the paper mentioned that he was a new recruit and that the outcome might have been different if he had been more experienced. Far from criticizing the game, the paper claimed that most injuries happened to those players who had not received "the right sort of training."[7] Similarly, when UK football player Harry Stevenson broke his leg in six places, effectively crippling him for life at a time when surgery to set bones was rare, the *Herald* did not blame the violence of football for the injury. It noted that the opponent who tackled Stevenson was taking part in his first game, and, in fact, his first tackle.[8]

The reader may well be struck by the primitive organization of sports on the campus during its earliest decades. On numerous occasions, the whole program seemed likely to collapse upon itself, largely because of a lack of money. Quite often the football team could not hire a coach until first playing several games and collecting the gate receipts. Almost every year, the future of the department depended on having a successful Thanksgiving Day game, which provided nearly all of its revenue. The lax, haphazard structure of the athletic department contrasts very sharply with the highly structured business that it is today. Indeed, if there were a "golden age of sports" at UK, it came after the period studied here.

During these first several decades, the UK program never caught up to the pioneers of college sports such as Harvard, Yale, and Princeton. These schools enjoyed a head start not only in their athletic departments but in the schools themselves. Harvard, for example, was founded more than two centuries before the University of Kentucky. As a result, they boasted an alumni base vastly larger than that of UK. Also, schools such as Columbia and the University of Pennsylvania had the advantage of being located in very large cities, which provided a much greater pool of ticket-buying spectators than available to a school tucked away in the heart of the Bluegrass.

Money fueled the sports program, and for the period studied

here, it was rarely in abundance. Sports at the University of Kentucky could not grow until permanent arenas were built giving the department access to increased gate receipts. The university was indeed very slow in building permanent facilities for its sports teams. Harvard started the stadium building craze in 1903 when it constructed a steel and concrete facility that seated forty thousand fans. The other major sports powers quickly followed suit. At UK, however, the football team responded by building (and rebuilding) temporary bleachers for each important game. Once during a game, the bleachers collapsed, injuring several spectators. When the university finally started construction of a permanent stadium, in 1924, the plans called for a seating capacity of only 25,000. Even these plans proved to be too optimistic. The athletic department could raise enough money to build only six sections (of the sixteen planned), which seated only 10,400 fans. Once again, the athletic department resorted to temporary wooden bleachers to accommodate the occasional overflow crowd.

Basketball was hindered the most by the lack of a suitable arena. For nearly two decades, the team played in a gymnasium with no spectator seating. The relatively small size of the university delayed any expansion for several decades. Early, the student body numbered only a few hundred. By 1940, it totaled slightly more than five thousand. In the long run, alumni support proved to be the most critical force in the expansion of the program, but the school lacked a sufficient alumni base for many years.

Some issues pertaining to the subject of sports at UK I have not attempted to address, or have touched on only lightly. For the entire period studied here, the university remained an all-white institution. Thus, I have not dealt with the issue of race in this work. I do, however, address gender issues (focusing on the beginnings of women's sports and the campaign to ban it). Also omitted are detailed references to what were referred to then as "the minor sports": baseball and track. Football was the major sport and, in fact, the only viable, self-sustaining sport. It produced nearly all the money, influenced nearly all the decisions, and it seemed, caused all the trouble. Even basketball, now the university's most famous sport, existed only as an adjunct of football. It was coached by football coaches and played primarily by football players. Even when basketball rose to prominence under Adolph Rupp, it did not generate enough money to declare its independence. During these early years, Rupp also served as an assistant football coach. As indicated by a 1931 audit, the athletic department earned $140,916.83. Of that amount football accounted for 64 percent, student fees 18 percent, basketball 6 percent, and the state high school basketball tournament 6 percent. Track and baseball combined accounted for only 1 percent of the year's total receipts.[9]

What remains is the story of an athletic program that struggled mightily for nearly a half a century and somehow managed to survive the many calamities that befell it, including those it brought upon itself. After World War II, the University of Kentucky sports program began to develop into one of the nation's finest. In doing so, it did not build upon its earlier legacy. If anything, the athletic department could not grow until it had escaped from the quagmire of its past.

THE ARRIVAL OF
FOOTBALL ON CAMPUS

*The game of football as at present played by so-called college
teams is brutal, dangerous, and not calculated to elevate the moral
character of the students.*

—UK board of trustees[1]

COLLEGE FOOTBALL came to Kentucky relatively late. As sports historian Ronald Smith has noted, the game had its roots in the hazing and initiation rites imposed upon freshmen at some northeastern schools as early as the 1850s. Alarmed by the violence and brutality associated with football, the faculty at schools such as Harvard, Yale, Brown, and West Point voted to ban the ritual. The game would be reborn later in the nineteenth century. Rutgers and Princeton played the first intercollegiate football game in 1869. In the 1870s, Columbia, Cornell, Penn, Harvard, and Yale adopted the sport.[2]

In 1924, the University of Kentucky student newspaper, the *Kernel*, curious as to football's origins in the state, conducted research and interviewed alumni. The paper reported that a group of Transylvania University students owned the first football ever seen in the Bluegrass. In the spring of 1880, the Transylvania students read a magazine advertisement describing the game. Pooling their resources, they raised the necessary six dollars and ordered a football and a rule book from a Philadelphia firm. They organized a team and played among themselves.[3]

The *Kernel's* version did not agree with one printed in the Transylvania college paper eight years earlier. The *Crimson Rambler* reported that Transylvania students played a version of the game in

7

the spring of 1879. They were led by C.L. Thurgood, a divinity student and native of Australia, who had played on a football team in Ballarat, a city near Melbourne. Responding to a challenge issued to Centre College (which had also adopted the sport), Transylvania played its first intercollegiate football game in 1880 under rules that more closely resembled soccer than either football or rugby. For this contest, the teams employed a round ball, which they kicked, being forbidden by the rules at that time to run with the ball. The *Lexington Daily Transcript* estimated that five hundred spectators watched the game. Some scholars have written that this contest was the first intercollegiate football game ever played in the South, and perhaps the first played west of the Alleghenies.[4]

In his history of the University of Kentucky, James F. Hopkins recorded that the following year the Transylvania students played three games with the students of the University of Kentucky a few blocks further south in the city. During the rest of the decade, the university students played a few other games at odd intervals.[5] Little is known of these contests. Lexington newspapers did not always take notice, and the university had neither yearbooks nor student newspapers during this period. As described by a later yearbook, athletics "had no special management," and teams were assembled "by some enthusiast and managed in a sort of pell-mell manner."[6] In 1892, after years of such haphazard efforts, the students determined to make a more concerted effort to field a team. That spring, they formed the student athletic association, adopting the common model used by many northeastern schools. Under this format, the affairs of the team became the responsibility of a manager elected by the student body and a captain chosen by team members. Also at this time the students chose the school's official team colors. At a chapel service in 1892, the students discussed several color combinations, including blue and yellow, which some football team members had used the previous year. Richard Stoll, a UK student and football player at this time (later a very prominent member of the school's board of trustees), was wearing a blue and white necktie that day. As he later recalled, he took it off and held it up, and from that day on the school's colors have been blue and white.[7]

The team suffered greatly both from a lack of knowledge of the game and from a lack of money. To alleviate these problems, the students chose the new geology professor, Arthur M. Miller, as manager. They were, it appears, operating on the assumption that because the young Miller was "an old Princeton man" he surely knew something about the game. Miller had not played the game at Princeton but had been an avid fan. He also had some coaching experience, having once tried to teach the game at a girls' school in Pennsylvania. As the new UK coach, Miller taught his new charges "the use of signals and hammered into their heads some knowledge of the game." More important, he advanced the necessary money to purchase uniforms and equipment.[8]

Students (especially those from the engineering department) enclosed a field to play on and built wooden bleachers. They were, however, able to proceed only after relocating the cows belonging to university president James Kennedy Patterson. Midway through the season, the team's prospects brightened even further when they procured a coach, John A. Thompson, who did in fact know the game, having played for Purdue. The team played six games with local colleges and athletic clubs, winning two. In 1893, the team posted its first winning season, and the students declared that everything looked bright for the future.[9]

For the next several decades, the athletic program was beset by problems. The most persistent difficulty was with finances. The students provided the sole force in both developing and supporting sports teams. Financial support came from athletic association dues. At some schools, pressure to join the association was so strong that it bordered on extortion. Dues were then augmented by fund-raising drives and gate receipts.[10]

The University of Kentucky sports program endured many financial hardships not borne by other, more prominent schools. It lacked the alumni base enjoyed by the eastern schools, which had a twenty-year head start in football. Its student body at this time numbered only about three hundred. Although the football team did possess a playing field, it lacked a true stadium. The bleachers provided only limited

A.M. Miller, geology professor
and one-time football coach

seating, and most spectators had to stand along the sidelines. Such an arrangement precluded a large paying crowd. As a result, the university athletic program never collected the large gate receipts or student membership dues that fueled the successful Ivy League teams. Harvard could boast of game-day crowds of 40,000; UK routinely drew crowds numbering only 150. Muckraking journalists could accuse the Yale athletic association of hiding a $100,000 slush fund; UK often could not afford to hire a coach or outfit all of its players with sufficient equipment.[11]

For many decades, the football team's financial problems proved so severe that the program threatened to collapse at any moment. Yet in the 1890s, another problem provided a greater crisis. The year 1893 brought not only the first winning season, but also the first rumblings of disapproval from the school's administration. The ambiguous, unofficial status of sports on the college grounds coupled with the violent aspects of football in particular disturbed the board of trustees and the university president. Dismayed by this lack of control, Patterson and

President James K. Patterson

the board passed a resolution placing the student-run athletic association under the jurisdiction of the faculty. The board further stipulated that the association should submit a constitution for board approval. The association failed to comply, and the following year the board took stronger action, placing several restrictions on campus sports.

To begin with, the board ruled that members of any UK athletic team must be "bona fide matriculates of the school of freshman rank or above." This effectively eliminated students from the college-based normal school, the faculty, and, most important, outside semiprofessional players that were becoming common at some eastern colleges. Moreover, the board pronounced that all student athletes must obtain faculty consent and "maintain a credible class standing." Any student not meeting these requirements would be required to withdraw from the athletic association. The board empowered its executive committee to make all such decisions.[12]

President Patterson believed that these measures, while perhaps steps in the right direction, did not go far enough. In addition to the board's concern for proper supervision, Patterson had deeper objections to sports. He stated that "the workings of the athletic association" were "not satisfactory and not conducive to the best interests of this institution." He persuaded the board to consider harsher sanctions, and thus the matter was referred to the committee on college discipline.[13]

In Patterson's thinking, football was no different than the other forms of campus violence that he so earnestly wanted to eradicate. He believed that the brutality involved in such activities as football, hazing, and class fights (especially the annual flag rush between the freshmen and sophomore classes) reflected badly on the entire university. Despite his efforts to eliminate violence on campus, the last years of the nineteenth century and the first years of the twentieth saw numerous incidents that generated the bad publicity that he detested. Twice during the 1890s, students viciously attacked the people charged with collecting dorm rent. On one occasion, a student in arrears stabbed and killed the rent agent. Shortly thereafter, a student shot and critically wounded another collector. At the time of the shooting, Patterson found himself in such close proximity that he disarmed the assailant, who then fled, never to be brought to justice.[14]

Patterson guarded the school's reputation with a zeal that frequently intimidated those around him. He was especially vocal in criticizing the faculty for not following his strict example. According to Patterson, the "laxness of discipline" that sometimes turned violent stemmed from the failure of the faculty to attend chapel and "to admonish and rebuke idle students." In 1902, one faculty member did attempt such a course of action with disastrous results. One night, the commandant of the college brigade (the forerunner of ROTC), Major McKee, attempted to investigate a firecracker incident in the dorm that he supervised. While he was questioning the students, the dorm lights mysteriously went out. Some of the dorm residents took advantage of the darkness and beat the despised commandant rather severely. The episode incensed Patterson, and although he sought no disciplinary charges against the students, he relieved McKee of all duties. Then, in typical fashion, Patterson took command of the dorm himself. At about the same time, Patterson also became dissatisfied with the discipline imposed upon the university's women students. To remedy this situation he appointed his brother, Walter Kennedy Patterson, as "dormitory matron." This appointment prompted many students to refer to the brothers secretly as "He-Pat" and "She-Pat."[15]

Patterson's critics often assailed him as a despot who ran the college as if it were personally his. In many ways it was. On more than one occasion, he saved the school from destruction. In 1878, for example, the state legislature dissolved the tie between Transylvania and its Agricultural and Mechanical extension, which later became the University of Kentucky. Buoyed by optimism and a state construction grant, the new college secured land at its current location and began construction in 1880. It soon became horrifyingly clear, however, that the allocation for the new buildings was inadequate. Late in 1881, the university hovered near bankruptcy. Because of expensive delays and the need to rebid contracts when the original contractors abandoned work, the buildings were only half completed.[16] Unable to petition the legislature for more money, Patterson and key board members appealed to numerous local and regional banks for a loan. The banks roundly refused, stating that the college had no securities to offer and that they indeed believed that "the whole will collapse like an eggshell." Undaunted, Patterson took the only course he saw open. He took out a personal loan, pledging his own life savings as collateral.[17]

The life of Patterson and the university were so closely entwined that one cannot be fully considered without the other. Some would say that after the death of his son in 1895, the university became his consuming passion. He served as president for forty-one years, a tenure unmatched by any of his contemporaries in the realm of academe. Moreover, it could well be argued that he was the most active president the university would ever know. In addition to his presidential duties he also served as the secretary of the board of trustees and the executive committee. He employed no secretary for thirty-five years, preferring to draft all of his own correspondence. In addition, he served as the business agent and registrar, paying all the university's bills and scheduling classes for all students himself. For forty-five years, he maintained a full teaching load as professor of history. He even appointed himself as superintendent of buildings and grounds and could be seen watering the trees on campus. After his retirement in 1910, he continued to sit on the board, even after the board tried to end that arrangement. Ignoring many requests, he refused to vacate the presidential house, forcing the new president and his wife to live in a dorm apartment. Upon his death in 1922, he made the university his principal heir.[18]

Clearly, Patterson had determined to defend the university against anything he thought might tarnish its reputation. Assured that his stand against football was morally correct and in the best interest of his university, he eagerly looked forward to the report of the committee on college discipline. In typically slow fashion, the committee did not report for twelve months. At that time, it proclaimed its support for the president, stating that it found "the game of football as at present played by so-called college teams" to be brutal, dangerous, and "not calculated to elevate the moral character" of the students. They recommended that the game be banned.[19] Rather than taking immediate action, the board voted to refer the matter to yet another subcommittee, which reported at the next trustees meeting six months later that it too approved of the restrictions prescribed earlier.[20]

The board's slow decision-making process gave the students ample time to prepare a desperate peace offering. Speed was critical, for if the students waited for the next trustee meeting in six months, a whole football season would be lost and Patterson might gain insurmountable momentum. The very next day, therefore, a committee of students petitioned the board to reinstate football. In support of their request, they presented a list of proposed rules to govern athletics. In essence, they were finally providing the constitution that the board had requested years earlier. Specifically, the students suggested that:

1. There shall be five members of the faculty who shall have control of all athletics in the college.
2. These five, plus four students, shall compose the Board of Directors of the Athletic Association.
3. Managers of the Athletic teams—football, baseball, and track—must be elected by the Athletic Association and approved by the faculty.
4. Managers must have the approval of the committee from the faculty before arranging any games with other teams to be played out of Lexington.
5. Any student in or above the Grade of Freshman who has a class standing above 11.25 [on the fifteen point grading scale, this would be roughly a C+ average] in each of his classes shall have the privilege to play on any team of the college in match games with other teams.
6. Any one in the college whose average class-standing is above 11.25 shall have the privilege to play in practice games among students of the institutions provided the Athletic Committee of the Faculty does not decide that it is interfering with his class-work.
7. No professional athletes and no one who is not a bona fide student shall play on any teams of this college.
8. Board of Directors shall have charge of the Athletic Grounds and shall be responsible to the College for their condition.
9. The Faculty may prohibit athletics among the students of this institution at any time.

This proposal pacified many board members who had objected not to sports in general but to the lack of administrative control over them. Much to Patterson's dismay, the board promptly reversed its stand and lifted the one-day ban. Surprised by this distinct lack of support, Patterson acquiesced without further protest.[21]

Although defeated for the moment, Patterson did not give up

hope that he could ban athletics. In addition to his disapproval of the violence associated with football, he did not think that time could be found in the students' daily schedule for any sport. Indeed, the routine set forth by Patterson left little time for anything, and during the nineteenth century there was virtually no social life at all on the campus. On any given weekday, students marched through the following strict regimen:

5:30	Reveille
6:30	Breakfast
7:30-8:30	Morning study
8:30	Chapel
9:00-12:00	Classroom recitation
12:00-1:00	Lunch
1:00-4:00	Afternoon study
4:00-5:00	Military drill
5:00-6:30	Supper
6:30-9:30	Evening study
10:00	Taps

There was practically no time for any student activities. From 5:30 A.M. to 10:00 P.M., students could claim only the time allotted for lunch and supper for themselves.[22]

The only approved extracurricular activities came in the form of literary and oratorical societies. Patterson feared that if students spent their scarce leisure time playing sports, their education would suffer. It should also be noted that Patterson was not critical of sports only but of nearly all extracurricular activities. In 1894, for example, he also recommended that the board refer the entire matter of fraternities to the committee on college discipline for possible sanctions. He also opposed school dances, and during the nineteenth century there were none on campus.[23]

Patterson's schedule may have been unduly harsh, but it reflected his own dour and autocratic personality. In addition, he was a deeply religious man who had attended seminary and had once planned for a career in the ministry. This background led him to believe that only strict discipline could save his students from being led down the wrong path to ruin and disgrace. He believed that if students enjoyed too much free time, they would fall prey to the "allurements of the city." He greatly feared the enticements provided by the city saloons and their free lunches, as well as gambling parlors and houses of prostitution "where both body and soul were wrecked by lascivious indulgences." The administration dealt harshly with any student caught visiting such forbidden places. It was even rumored (correctly so, as it is now known) that Patterson employed spies to gather his off-campus information.[24]

It was not uncommon for college administrators to be so concerned with student activities. Indeed, most nineteenth-century faculties took their responsibilities of in loco parentis very seriously. In the words of a Princeton professor, "every professor should feel it to be his duty to look after the morals and behavior of the students in the classroom, chapel, and elsewhere."[25] At Kentucky, Patterson attempted to impose his harsh disciplinarian personality upon the entire campus. Defending his beliefs, he told the board that students while at the university were their wards and that the board had an unshakable obligation to look after and to conserve their morals. Patterson urged that the administration must "throw every safeguard around them and take all available measures to prevent them from falling into lascivious habits."[26]

It is not surprising, therefore, that Patterson and the board spent hours discussing all aspects of student life. The board went so far as to note in the official university minutes which students should be reprimanded for not making their beds. The board stayed quite busy reviewing such matters because the code of student conduct devised by Patterson contained nearly two hundred rules. Rule 99, for example, required all students "to attend divine services at least once every Sunday." According to Rule 129, they could not have any printed material, newspaper, magazine, or book in their room without the permission of the president. Nor could they (Rule 75) have a discussion among themselves that contained any criticism of the faculty or administration.[27]

If only for the moment, football had escaped Patterson's zeal for rigid discipline and conformity. It was in essence a narrow escape, and few observers doubted that the president would soon renew his attacks on campus sports. Meanwhile, sports at the university still struggled to maintain even a tenuous existence. Events of the next few years revealed that the whole college athletic program teetered on the brink of collapse.

Throughout much of central Kentucky, college football exhibited a haphazard organization. Schools often began the season still trying to schedule opponents. They frequently canceled and rescheduled games at the very last moment. The most extreme case of a late cancellation occurred when Vanderbilt called off their game with Transylvania after the latter had boarded the train for Nashville. This cancellation nearly devastated the team's yearly budget. Their funds were so low to start with that they had borrowed $100 from a sympathetic professor to pay for the $102.70 train fare. The team hoped to repay the loan with the money made in Nashville. Vanderbilt had promised the Crimson a $100 appearance fee plus a share of the gate receipts.[28]

It would be years before all rules were standardized. Meanwhile, the competing schools were left to work out acceptable rules of play that might vary from week to week. Sometimes the teams played two thirty-minute halves, sometimes the halves lasted twenty or twenty-five minutes. Sometimes the second half was shorter that the first. On some occasions, bad weather prompted the teams to quit midway into the game.[29] As a result of this lack of uniformity, constant disagreements marked the games of the 1890s. On one occasion, the argument (over how a penalty was to be enforced) became so fierce that Transylvania walked off the field in protest, forfeiting the game to UK. Similarly, the Newcastle-Centre game also broke up in a fierce dispute over a play that Centre thought should have tied the score. While the teams argued, the spectators spilled onto the field and refused to let the game continue.[30]

The question of player eligibility caused the greatest commotion. In the absence of an effective governing body, the competing schools had to settle the issue of eligibility between themselves each week.

Sometimes this proved to be quite difficult. One Transylvania-University of Kentucky game started twenty minutes late because the teams argued over the eligibility of each other's players. The 1896 game between Central University and the Lexington Athletic Club (LAC) almost collapsed minutes before kickoff. The LAC protested Central's lineup, claiming that it "had an agreement with the CU boys that none but college men should play and a further agreement that Billy Lyons [CU coach] should not play." The "long-haired warriors from Richmond," however, insisted that they would not play unless Lyons played. In response the LAC captain, Wallace Muir, announced to the crowd that they could receive a refund at the gate. With their bluff called, CU agreed to banish their coach to the sideline. It is doubtful that his absence on the field hindered them any as they defeated LAC handily, 22-5.[31]

Often the season was made or broken before the first game even began. The biggest problem faced by the UK team involved finding enough money to hire a coach. More often than not in the 1890s, the team could not afford this luxury and consequently found it difficult to compete against professionally coached opponents. After the team's 32-0 loss to Centre College in 1896, the *Herald* noted that Centre exhibited such superior teamwork and scientific play because they had an excellent coach whereas UK had none.[32] Sometimes the team had to play several games and hope that the gate receipts and campus fundraisers generated enough revenue to pay for a coach.

The 1897 season began in typical fashion. In late September, the *Herald* wrote that the UK manager was corresponding furiously with eastern schools and hoped to have a coach at an early date. Things actually worked out better than in some years, and the team succeeded in hiring Lyman Eaton, former captain of the University of Cincinnati football squad. He arrived in Lexington just before the first game of the season. Before that time, the team captain had been in charge of coaching the team and choosing the players.[33] Any optimism generated by Eaton's hiring quickly evaporated. Greatly discouraged by a lack of practice time, adequate equipment, and financial support, the team announced that it would disband. The walkout lasted ten days. On October 20, the *Herald* announced that Eaton had been able to reunite the team, except for the two starting running backs, who refused to resume training. With this "late misunderstanding with the faculty" put aside, the team proceeded to post a dismal record. The disgruntled team won twice while losing four games in which they did not score.[34]

Saddled with primitive facilities, a chronic lack of revenue, and a hostile administration, the future looked bleak for the fledgling athletic program. Yet, out of the dark legacy of 1897 came one of the most storied seasons in UK history. It could well be argued that the most promising development in the early evolution of sports at the university took place a month after the close of the 1897 season. It occurred away from the playing field and may have gone unnoticed by most supporters of UK athletics. On January 2, 1898, Governor William O. Bradley appointed twenty-two-year-old Richard C. Stoll to the UK board of trustees. The nomination of such a young person to the board was unprecedented, but Stoll had the advantage of belonging to a very highly-placed political family (as well as Lexington's wealthiest family). The Stoll family controlled companies known today as Kentucky Utilities, GTE, Columbia Gas, First Security National Bank, and Kentucky American Water. The Stolls also had holdings in railroads and distilleries, and eventually acquired both city newspapers—the *Leader* in 1914 and the *Herald* in 1937. Richard Stoll entered the University of Kentucky in 1891 and played halfback on the football team. After graduating in 1895, he attended Yale Law School, earning a degree in 1897. He returned to Lexington, where he practiced law and could be seen attending local football games, occasionally serving as a college football referee.[35]

With the exception of a single three-year hiatus, he served on the board until his death in 1949. For thirty years he chaired the executive committee and frequently served on the committee for college discipline. He became a very powerful board member and a worthy adversary for Patterson. He arrived at a time when campus sports certainly needed a friend in high places. As one of his first official acts as a trustee, he moved that the board appropriate two hundred dollars to the athletic association. He found no support for his motion.[36]

UK trustee Richard C. Stoll

The rest of 1898 proved to be more successful. In fact the Blue and White team that season reached legendary status, finishing undefeated and unscored-upon. Despite its eventual renown, the season did not begin all that auspiciously. The UK team once again began the season without a coach, Lyman Eaton having fled the sinking ship after the dismal 1897 campaign. The football manager had scheduled crosstown rival Transylvania for the first game in hopes that the event would attract enough students and townspeople to swell the gate receipts and provide enough revenue to hire a coach.[37] Unfortunately, the weather conspired against them. As the *Leader* explained, "the day was too warm for vigorous exercise," and although the Blue and White proved victorious by an 18-0 score, only two hundred spectators witnessed the game. Furthermore, the heat prompted the teams to shorten the second half to fifteen minutes.[38]

Even a lopsided victory the next week over Georgetown did not generate much optimism. The *Leader* sharply criticized both teams, claiming that neither squad showed any of the teamwork needed to have a real football team. Despite the one-sided nature of the game, the sloppy play revealed that UK desperately needed a coach.[39] Several more weeks passed before the athletic association coffers permitted them to hire a replacement for Eaton. Once more, the team persuaded a former University of Cincinnati captain to take the helm. Shortly before the October 29 game against the Louisville Athletic Club, new coach W.R. Bass arrived in Lexington.[40]

The LAC team outweighed its opponent by fifty pounds per man and entered the game the clear favorite. The outcome surprised the crowd as UK won 17-0, demonstrating that skill could outplay brawn. The *Leader* also believed that the victory proved the value of a good coach. It predicted that if Bass were given the proper encouragement by the students and faculty, he would make the team the best in the state.[41] The season's outcome fulfilled the newspaper's prophecy. Although the opponents always seemed much heavier, the Blue and White team won every game by virtue of their superior training. Sports writers described the last game of the season as "the prettiest game of the season." Exhibiting the best teamwork ever seen in the state, UK trounced the Newcastle Athletic Club by the score of 36-0. Richard Stoll umpired the contest.[42]

The season did, however, have its share of minor disappointments. It was not a very profitable season. The early (pre-Bass) games attracted very small crowds. Most important, several highly anticipated (and potentially lucrative) games with major rivals never materialized. For example, the students and townspeople eagerly looked forward to the November 16 game with Centre College that the newspaper declared would decide the state championship. Shortly before halftime of that game, with UK a few feet short of the Centre goal, Centre refused to line up for the next play. Its players walked off the field, claiming that the incessant rain had made the field too muddy to play. The UK manager tried to reschedule the game, but all attempts failed.[43]

Compounding this disappointment, the team manager announced that despite weeks of negotiations with teams from Ohio, Tennessee, and West Virginia, he had been unable to schedule a game for Thanksgiving Day. With no game to see in town, many fans traveled (taking

"The Immortals" of 1898, undefeated and unscored upon. Coach W.R. Bass (back row) is pictured wearing his University of Cincinnati sweater.

their ticket money with them) to see the University of Cincinnati play the Carlisle Indian Academy. Many others made the short trip to Richmond to watch the Central University-Centre College clash.[44]

The final financial disappointment of the season came when Central's manager wrote that his team had suffered too many injuries in the Centre game and would not be able to play UK the next week as scheduled.[45] The cancellation of these games dealt a sharp blow to the team's financial condition, especially when combined with the poor attendance at the early games. The largest crowd of the year totaled only four hundred, an improvement over some years but a crowd no larger than typical for a Patterson Literary Society contest.[46] Despite these letdowns, the students declared the season an unparalleled success. The team had won seven games and lost none. It had scored 180 points while yielding none. After the Thanksgiving recess, the students and the faculty gave "a grand reception in honor of the team." From that time on, central Kentuckians would refer to the team of '98 as "the Immortals."[47]

In spite of such adoration, it was still abundantly clear that the university football program maintained only a tenuous existence at best. It was plagued by financial problems, opposition from the administration, and scheduling difficulties. As the century drew to a close, the sport faced an uncertain future. Events of the next decade would greatly test the foundations of the still-evolving athletic program. Before long, the football team would have its first brush with scandal, prompting Patterson to renew his campaign to ban all sports on campus.

THE FIRST
ATHLETIC SCANDAL

I believe this game or any game containing elements of danger
is necessary to the development of young men.
　　　—James R. Day, chancellor of Syracuse University[1]

ALTHOUGH NEVER QUITE MATCHING the perfect record of the
Immortals, the university football team continued its winning ways
into the new century. Once a mediocre team, UK now routinely beat
old foes such as Centre and Central. In 1900, it was the only team to
beat the powerful Louisville Athletic Club.[2] This turnaround was not
lost on the university's opponents. As early as 1898, Transylvania had
accused UK of playing semiprofessionals, or "ringers," as these nonstudents were commonly called.[3]

　　As the Thanksgiving game between UK and Transylvania became
more popular with the citizens of Lexington, the rivalry between the
two schools became increasingly bitter. The game had become the
highlight of the college sports season and the remedy to the teams'
financial woes. Football teams, especially the major northeastern powers, generally made more money from this game than from any other
source. The president of Lafayette College once noted that the holiday contest generated more revenue than the rest of the college spent
in a year.[4]

　　With each passing year, more accusations began to fly that one
Lexington team or the other had been hiring professionals to play in
the holiday event. Mindful of its shaky relationship with the administration, UK athletic association director W.H. Kiler tried to dismis the
charges. He stated that the university would always stand for purity in

athletics. He assured everyone that each member of the Blue and White was indeed "a student and a gentleman who had won his position by hard work and who knew that he must keep up his studies." Employing a local metaphor, he promised that as surely "as the Kentucky horse surpassed all others in speed, beauty, and endurance, so too the athletics of Kentucky would surpass those of other states."[5]

Rumors of scandals past and impending did not escape Patterson's attention. Although still nursing serious reservations about the place of athletics in higher education, he had remained quiet since 1896. He broke his silence during his regular address to the board of trustees in July 1903. He told the assembled trustees that he still believed that sports interfered "very seriously with study and the duties of the classroom." He complained that during baseball and football seasons, students neglected their studies to prepare for the match games. Shifting his emphasis, he insisted that if sports were to continue on campus, then the existing rules must be strictly applied. He reminded the board that all athletes must be "bona fide college matriculates" and not professionals, as he feared were being hired by some schools to ensure victory.[6] The events that followed confirmed his greatest fears. The 1903 football season exploded in controversy, and the fallout endured for several years. So great was the rift that grew between the two local schools that they discontinued the popular holiday game. For a while, it appeared that the local universities would ban all athletics.

In addition to rumors, a tremendous amount of anticipation and press coverage preceded the 1903 Thanksgiving game. On November 1, the *Herald* noted that college football in Kentucky had never been "free from the taint of professionalism." Once again, both teams charged that the other was "composed in the main of ringers." The paper lamented that if this trend filtered downward, eligibility rules would have to be implemented "to preserve the integrity of kindergarten ring-around-the-rosey." The article decreed that if the sport could not be kept above suspicion, it should be abolished.[7]

As Thanksgiving approached, both schools continued to use the newspaper as a forum for their charges against each other. Some observers speculated that the game might be canceled. In one of the longest articles ever printed in the *Herald,* every aspect of the growing controversy received careful scrutiny. The original contract between the schools (signed April 18, 1903) specified the date, time, and place for the game. It also provided that the schools would share the gate receipts equally. Continuing a tradition, the agreement called for both team managers to exchange lineups. These rosters were to contain the names of all players who had been deemed eligible by the faculty of their schools.[8]

Problems arose when the University of Kentucky athletic association refused to honor this tradition. The association explained that because of the "rather loose sentiment prevailing in our community concerning athletics," the exchange of lists had become entirely meaningless as a way of attesting to the character of the players. It accused Transylvania of being "in a large measure responsible" for this attitude and stated further that it would not give sanction to a custom that had been repeatedly and flagrantly violated by nearly all the colleges of the state.

Moreover, the association claimed that Transylvania had violated "the original spirit and the intention of the contract" when it refused to join the new regulatory body, the Kentucky Intercollegiate Athletic Association (KIAA). Because of this development, it did not believe it was "bound by any rule or regulations that ordinarily governed leagues or associations."[9]

The Transylvania athletic association replied that the game contract had been signed four months before the formation of the KIAA. It insisted that UK submit its roster "to prevent a repetition of the events of last Thanksgiving" when a number of UK players had entered the college only a week before the game and then left Lexington immediately after the game. Transylvania believed that UK's refusal to submit its list only added credibility to the rumors that its coach (C.A. Wright, a former Columbia star) had traveled to New York to sign players.[10]

UK quickly denied these allegations. Taking the offensive, it accused Transylvania of playing two ringers under assumed names in the recent game with the University of Virginia. The UK athletic association also claimed that it was widely known that the Crimson football team had played two professional baseball players for the entire season. On this point, the *Herald* took sides. It noted that the rules against professionalism should not apply to Transylvania's Yancey brothers. Hogan and Worth Yancey had, in fact, played summer baseball for money, but only to help pay their college expenses. As the paper described, this rule was a technical one used by eastern colleges to keep professional baseball players out of college baseball and should not be applied to amateur football. After all, the *Herald* reminded its readers, the Yanceys were indeed bona fide students.[11]

Apart from that one indulgence, the paper criticized both colleges. The *Herald* explained that the person who played the game of football unfairly would ultimately play the game of life dishonestly. As such, the schools set a very bad example for the state's youths. The paper believed that the teams should heed the example of the local horse racing industry. There, the person who entered a ringer was forever barred from the track. It was time, the article concluded, for football to be played fairly or to be banned entirely.[12]

Two days later, the *Herald* reported that in spite of the difficulties, the teams would play. UK still refused to submit a list of its players, but Transylvania had dropped its demand. The new proposition, the paper described, was "bring on your team and no questions will be asked." Local enthusiasts greatly welcomed this latest agreement. The paper hoped that the game would be clean and free from unfair play, while warning that any roughness, whether from players or spectators, would be dealt with severely.[13]

As the date of the game drew near, excitement in Lexington reached a fever pitch. The *Herald* commented that no other recent event had generated more interest in the city than the impending contest. More money had also been bet on the game than ever before. Kentucky was running a 10-7 underdog, though some even-money bets could be found. Interest was not strictly confined to Lexington. Fans from Danville, Mt. Sterling, Paris, Lawrenceburg, Nicholasville, and Winchester chartered special trains for the event. The paper predicted that if the weather cooperated, 3,500 people would attend. To accommodate the expected crowd, UK had constructed two grand-stands, each ninety feet long. The admission price jumped from the usual 50 cents to $1.25, and an additional 50 cents would be charged to park a carriage. As an extra precaution, the mayor assigned twenty-five police officers to patrol the game.[14]

Speculation over the teams' lineups, charges, and countercharges continued. The *Herald* claimed that both teams had "ample emergency timber." Every hour brought fresh new rumors of husky gridiron war-riors wending their way stealthily to one practice field or the other. Stories abounded that both colleges had been scouring the country in search of "suitable material." Transylvania continued to assert that all of its players had played for the team throughout the entire season.[15] The next day, it changed its story slightly, admitting that it did in fact have new men in practice but would only use them if it found itself outplayed by UK's ringers.[16]

As reported by the *Herald,* the results of the long-awaited game did a great deal to vindicate Transylvania and vilify UK. Not only did Transylvania win handily 17-0, but the paper stated that the victory was "all the more sweet" because the Crimsons had played the entire contest without a single change in its lineup. Furthermore, the men who played had been with the team all year long. On the other hand, only two regular-roster players could be found on the UK team—the rest apparently gathered from different parts of the country. The *Her-ald* claimed that Kentucky's team boasted several players from Centre College and at least five strangers from New York City. The northern contingent included college and professional players and at least "one alleged pugilist." Despite such extreme efforts, UK lost the game badly, crossing midfield only once and never threatening to score. This poor performance led spectators on both sides to believe that the result would have been better if UK had played its own players. The team had in fact entered the contest undefeated.[17]

In reviewing the 1903 season, the *Herald* could point to few high-lights from around the state. It briefly recounted football's demise at Centre College. After three games, the faculty and administra-tion there became so angered that they successfully banned the sport in mid-season. In general, the paper condemned the football season as being marked by the struggle between pure athletics and ringerism, stating that in the last game of the season, "the cause of pure athletics received a decided check by the importation of hired players by one college."[18]

The UK college yearbook also reviewed the season. It reported that the athletic agreements between various colleges were laxly observed and as a result professionalism tainted sports "in more than one institution." This was clearly evident in the 1903 season, which saw one college team disbanded on account of ringers, another play professionals throughout the season, and a third one import "a number of false alarms for the biggest game of the season." The yearbook staff did not name these institutions.[19] In spite of such downplayed scandals, the yearbook proclaimed that athletics "even when viewed in a most conservative light are in a very flourishing condition." It described football as the one feature of undergraduate life that did more for a college than any other. It created a common cause and brought the faculty and students together. Far from criticizing the team for the ringer controversy, the yearbook pronounced that the team should be admired and cherished. It should even be ranked alongside the Immortals of '98.[20]

On the administrative level, President Patterson did not share this rosy evaluation. Furious over the allegations of scandal, he requested a thorough investigation. The appointed committee prepared its report slowly. Not until June 1904 did the board hear from the special committee on athletics. Much to Patterson's dismay, the committee reported that their evidence confirmed the earlier charges that both the athletic association and the faculty had recruited ringers for the Thanksgiving game. "It is manifest," the committee chair announced, that the faculty "schemed to import nine professional football players from New York City." It then paid these ringers from the gate receipts. The committee concluded that such actions brought reproach upon the university and that all involved in the scandal should be condemned.[21]

Other than firing the football coach, the board took no additional action on the matter. Yet events of that fall did nothing to alleviate the problem or lessen Patterson's ire. November arrived, and as always, the town's excitement grew. The *Herald* explained that anticipation had indeed gripped the citizens of Lexington. "No follower of horse racing," it noted, had "ever figured 'dope' more closely." The betting was very brisk, but this year there was no clear favorite and even-money bets prevailed. The two teams offered quite a contrast. Transylvania's team had a dramatic advantage in size while UK hoped to compensate with its superior speed.[22]

The University of Kentucky, still smarting from three successive losses in the big game took extra measures in 1904 to ensure victory. The newspaper commented that the team was well-rested. In fact, there had been several weeks during which UK had not played. The team had even refused an offer to play Catlettsburg "with a view to the Thanksgiving game." As a further precautionary measure, Coach Schacht confined his players to campus and made them eat all meals at a training table under his supervision. UK players pinned their hopes of victory on speed, although many critics believed they could not maintain it throughout the entire game.[23]

The newspaper was especially pleased to announce that, unlike the previous year, both teams had submitted their lists early. Both teams also indicated that they were satisfied that all proposed players were eligible. The *Herald* hoped that such an agreement would bring the two colleges together and subdue the growing bitterness of the rivalry.[24] These hopeful sentiments were quickly dashed. One day later, the *Herald* told its readers that despite earlier reports of agreement, the University of Kentucky planned to protest the eligibility of some Transylvania players.[25] Several days passed with no further communication between the two schools. Once again, rumors began to circulate that the holiday game might be canceled. In a November 21 article entitled "Shut Up and Play Ball," the *Herald* reprinted a letter from Transylvania's athletic committee. Its chair, Professor A.P. Fairhurst, complained that inevitably, UK's protests were never received until they had appeared in the paper. Fairhurst retorted, "in the name of honesty and peace and decency, we counsel you to cool off and quiet down."

Fairhurst reminded UK that under the constitution of the KIAA (which the school had joined since the previous season) all eligibility protests were to be decided by the faculty of the disputed players. This was the rule, and UK could either submit to it or refuse to play. In bitter sarcasm, Fairhurst declared that UK could bring any team its faculty would approve—even if the public knew that they were ringers. Even if UK played eleven ringers instead of only nine as it did last year, Transylvania would play. With growing acrimony, Fairhurst wrote that UK could again bring its team "from the four quarters of the earth and from the fifth quarter if you can find it." It could "gather them from all the tribes and kindred of the earth." If it so desired, it could bring "Hottentots, Flat-head Indians, Patagonians, Native Australians, Esquimaux, New Yorkers, Danvillians, Cincinnatians, Hoodoos, Burgoos, Whatnots, Topnots . . . the more the merrier," and Transylvania would play.[26]

The following day, the *Herald* reported a new development. In an article entitled "Protests are Erased From Slate—Game Will Be Played," the paper described the very recent meeting of the KIAA during which the league declared all disputed players eligible. All was not, however, completely peaceful. Once again, Transylvania's Fairhurst questioned the right of the KIAA to rule on any eligibility matters, claiming that Article 7, Section 4 of the KIAA constitution gave that right to the college faculty. In sharper language, he demanded to know why this "emergency meeting" had been called and by whom. The *Herald* reported that, oddly, the meeting had not been demanded by UK but rather by Centre College's faculty representative, A.H. Throckmorton, who would become Transylvania's most vocal antagonist. He had arranged the meeting to discuss the eligibility of several Crimson players, claiming that the school had been paying one of its players. He withdrew the charge after hearing a statement from the college treasurer.

Throckmorton next challenged another player's eligibility, claiming that he had enrolled at the college just in time to play against UK in the Thanksgiving game. Fairhurst explained that the athlete in question had enrolled late because he had been "delayed from entering college on account of a protracted meeting which he held." The KIAA greeted this explanation with suspicion, but ruled that because of a loophole in the league regulations, the player was eligible. Baseball, it noted, had an enrollment deadline, but not football. A student could, therefore, enter school the day before a game and play if he were properly registered for the equivalent of twelve hours per week.

The KIAA next entertained a third eligibility protest. UK claimed that a particular Transylvania football player was not a bona fide matriculate. Fairhurst informed the board that this student was in fact enrolled in the college's medical department and had been in attendance since April. UK then dropped the protest. Still not satisfied, Throckmorton requested that the board adopt rule changes and insisted that Transylvania forfeit its two previous victories over Centre. The KIAA chair ruled that such matters could not be discussed until the regular meeting in January. UK and Transylvania agreed not to lodge any further protests, and the meeting adjourned.[27]

After such wrangling, the game was almost anticlimactic. Thanks to its superior speed and superb conditioning, UK won handily, 21-4. Transylvania escaped a shutout only with a brilliant run by its star player. Despite the predictions of some observers, the Blue and White's "light team" lasted the entire game and outplayed Transylvania's larger but slower team. Coach Schacht (an ex-Columbia star himself) commented that his team had played as well as any of the more famous Eastern colleges.[28]

While perhaps avoiding the open scandals of the previous year, the 1904 football season was hardly a resounding success. It left behind a legacy of bitterness that only escalated over the course of the next year. In the fall of 1905, the UK-Transylvania rivalry erupted in its final controversy. It involved the administrations of several schools, led to rule changes, and brought an end to one of Lexington's most popular and eagerly anticipated sporting events.

As the 1905 installment of the Thanksgiving game approached, there appeared to be a lack of the usual excitement. The *Herald* did not describe brisk betting or changing odds, nor did it write about anticipated crowds or town excitement. This could have been owing in part to the tiresome difficulties of the past years. It could also have been attributed to the lackluster play of UK so far that season. On November 11, for example, the paper described an "awful drubbing" for the team that had just lost to St. Louis University by the lopsided score of 82-0.[29]

As the holiday neared, the interminable question of player eligibility popped up yet again. UK submitted its list of players early but stated in advance that it would challenge the eligibility of Transylvania's players. It wanted to convene an emergency meeting of the KIAA to settle the issue.[30] Once again, Transylvania questioned the right of the KIAA to rule on the matter, noting that there was no rule in the organization's constitution granting such power of review. That right was to be invested in the individual faculties. The only options open to an opposing team were to play or not to play.[31]

This time, the two schools were unable to resolve their differences. Unlike previous years, the teams had not signed the game contract the previous spring. A week before the game was to be played, UK returned the contract to Transylvania unsigned. Its spokesperson informed the *Herald* that the latest deadlock involved the choice of playing fields. The contract called for the game to be played at Transylvania. UK claimed that its field was so superior that the game could only be played there. For the first time in years, the paper concluded, it appeared that the breach had widened to the point that the game would not be played. It hinted that both colleges were considering playing other teams on Thanksgiving.[32]

The following day, UK issued another demand. Specifically, its athletic association demanded that Transylvania sign the contract and submit its list by 4:30 P.M. that day or cancel the game. The Transylvania football manager told the *Herald* that this ultimatum was not delivered to him until 2:45 P.M. and that it was impossible to comply within the remaining one hour and fifteen minutes. He assured the newspaper that his team was willing to play under any rules.[33]

The newspaper evaluated the impasse and once again sided with Transylvania. It noted that the game had been played on the UK campus every year except 1902, and thus Transylvania's request on that point was only fair. It also agreed that the KIAA had no right to rule on player eligibility. The paper fervently hoped that the game would be played fearing that the popularity of football would be impaired if the schools did not stop their quibbling.[34]

Over the course of the next week, relations among several Kentucky colleges deteriorated precipitously. Once again, Centre's A.H. Throckmorton led the offensive against Transylvania. On November 27, the *Herald* revealed that during the football season, Throckmorton had sent letters to Transylvania's opponents, warning them that the Crimson athletes were ringers. His allegations were familiar. As in the previous year, he accused the school of paying a player. He also claimed that Transylvania's star player, George Varnell, was in his seventh year of college football, having played three years at another college.[35]

In the next day's *Herald*, Throckmorton intensified his attacks. He claimed that the entire Transylvania faculty had committed a most flagrant breach of ethics by certifying its players as eligible. He further alleged that, since he had been in Kentucky, Transylvania had openly and shamelessly played ringers. He was outraged that the school administration had given its blessing to this disgraceful policy. Throckmorton promised that he was willing to spend years, if necessary, to find the evidence to prove his claims.[36]

In the same article, Lyman Chalkey, dean of the Transylvania Law School, answered Throckmorton's charges. The school had actually dealt with these same allegations before and had even been cleared by the KIAA earlier. Transylvania had provided proof that Varnell had only been in residence at the University of Chicago for one and one-half quarters, ending in 1904.[37] Chalkey replied that all other charges and allegations against Transylvania were mere rumors. He noted with some surprise that Throckmorton, a law school dean himself, would stoop to such a level. After all, courts existed to arrive at the truth and prevent injustice "whether it be intended by ignorance, jealousy, malice, or disappointment." He further maintained that courts would not allow rumors to be introduced as evidence. At least, he snidely concluded, that is what he taught in his law school. If the law were taught differently in Danville, Chalkey wanted to be so advised.[38]

On November 28, the *Herald* officially announced what many readers had dreaded. Page one headlines proclaimed that a "sharp exchange of charges" between the two colleges had ended all negotiations and the Thanksgiving game would definitely not be played. For the first time that season, Transylvania took the offensive, releasing the report of their own secret investigation into Kentucky's football program. The Transylvania athletic association presented the *Herald* with numerous sworn affidavits implicating UK in football fraud, including payments to players and the recruiting of ringers. The newspaper gave the University of Kentucky an opportunity to respond to these very explicit charges. Its athletic association merely replied that the allegations were disgraceful and maligned "young Kentucky boys of high standing and the best families."[39]

In typical fashion, the *Herald* again sided with Transylvania, stating that in "the judgement of the community," Transylvania occupied "the most advantageous position." Its offers to negotiate with UK were more than fair. The *Herald* also believed the Crimson team was much stronger than that of UK. The paper did note, however, that it regretted the actions of both schools. In its opinion, both colleges had "been guilty of practices which, if indulged in by horse trainers, would subject them to being ruled off the track for life." The article concluded that even though most Lexingtonians believed that football was the best game ever played at the college level, it would be better to "see it stopped altogether than to have such unseemly controversies every year."[40]

Many observers had speculated that both teams would schedule other opponents for Thanksgiving. The University of Kentucky did not. Its team elected a captain for the next season and then promptly disbanded. On the other hand, Transylvania was able to arrange a game with Ohio Wesleyan College. Although some critics believed that any quality opponent would have already booked a game for the holiday, the *Herald* tried to play up the caliber of the contest. They noted that Ohio Wesleyan had once defeated the famed Carlisle Indian Academy. In inflated rhetoric, it labeled this substitute game the "Battle of the Year."[41] Unfortunately, the contest did not live up to its billing.

Transylvania won easily by the score of 40-0, ending the season unbeaten. The paper estimated that 2,500 spectators attended the game, including about 400 UK students and the Blue and White football team, which cheered for their crosstown rival.[42]

The events of the preceding years left an indelible legacy on the athletic programs of the two colleges. Angered by the actions of the KIAA and those of Throckmorton, Transylvania withdrew (UK claimed it was expelled) from the organization. This effectively ended the popular Thanksgiving series as KIAA rules forbad a member team to play any nonmember.[43] The multiyear controversy also resulted in rule changes dealing with player eligibility. It seems evident that Transylvania did not actually violate the letter of the KIAA constitution. It did in fact register students late in the fall strictly to play football. Yet, under KIAA bylaws, this was legal, so long as the students registered for a full course load. As did some other schools, Transylvania occasionally "hid" late-registered students in the medical or law schools, which had different admission policies.[44] Comparatively, the rule violations of the University of Kentucky appeared more blatant, and on occasion, spectacular.

These actions prompted the KIAA to close the loopholes in its eligibility requirements. To do so, it adopted a residence requirement similar to that instituted by many northern schools a decade earlier. Referred to locally as the Rule of 1906, it provided that athletes could not play for a college in an intercollegiate game until they had attended that college for one year. The UK yearbook hoped that this new rule would develop great teams that would bring honor to the college and state.[45]

The football debacle of 1905 once again attracted the attention of the UK administration. President Patterson had remained uncharacteristically quiet since the summer of 1904. During that time his rage simmered. After the 1905 football season, he began to vent his fury in angry reports to the board of trustees. He may well have been emboldened by the absence of Richard Stoll from the board. In 1904, Stoll began a three-year leave of absence. In December, Patterson told the board that football had become the university's most trying problem. The notion of clean athletics had been "compromised to a degree that is to say the least of it perplexing and sometimes humiliating." As recent events had shown, athletic contests quickly degenerated into battles over ringers and opportunities for gamblers. Fueled by large sums of money, they became a disgraceful hindrance to academic progress.[46] As an outspoken critic of gambling, Patterson was clearly upset about newspaper articles stating that the betting on the Thanksgiving game was so heavy and widespread that even young girls had been wagering candy and white gloves.[47]

In his next address, he resumed his attack, stating that sports robbed students of study time. He noted that "practice for match games" made heavy demands on the students' time. Moreover, the games, "when played at a distance and in rapid succession by itinerant teams made deep inroads upon classroom work." Surely, the faculty and administration had a right to protect the students from such "dissipation of energy."[48] Patterson further stated that he did in fact favor exercise for the students. He believed that the college should retain "what is confessedly good in physical culture." But, he railed, such results were not best attained by the "violent, spasmodic, and abnormal exertions" of sports. He calculated that in nine cases out of ten, athletic achievements were of no lasting value and could never "compensate for the lost opportunities of scholarship and mental and moral and physical training for industrial leadership and for all the higher and nobler ends of human existence."[49]

In his December address, Patterson again protested that sports robbed the student-athlete of time that should be devoted to study, military drill, gymnastic training, and laboratory work. He also claimed that all students were similarly hindered because the athletic association frequently detained the entire student body after chapel "in order to work up an artificial interest for contributed money to meet expenses." As usual, he directed the full force of his wrath against football. According to Patterson, football's legacy was limited to broken noses, legs, and arms, wasted time, idleness, and "a heritage of demoralization." Such an atmosphere perverted the true purpose of a college education. He urged the board to take strong and decisive action.[50]

The board reconvened the following day and to Patterson's great delight reported that it agreed unanimously that intercollegiate games should be prohibited. Specifically, no team would be permitted "to go abroad to play," and outside teams would not be permitted upon the university grounds. Intramural games, however, could continue if properly regulated. In a measure that might have indicated the board's lack of unanimity, a motion was made and carried to appoint a subcommittee "to investigate the condition of college athletics and report next June."[51]

The intervening six months gave several key trustees time to gather support. Most notably, the appointment of the subcommittee delayed action long enough that by the time the board voted, Richard Stoll had resumed his board seat. At the much anticipated June meeting, Patterson began by stating that he believed that the instruction given by the physical education department in the gymnasium (a facility he had frequently praised) was sufficient for the college's needs. He then unexpectedly softened his attacks on sports, stating that "I do not propose or suggest that sports be forbidden; but I do insist that they should be limited within the bounds of expediency." He urged the board to limit the time allotted not only to athletics but also "to dances, and to all other kinds of amusements which dissipate energy, create habits of idleness, and wreck the serious business and purpose of life."[52] Unmoved, the subcommittee reported that a majority of its members recommended that the college permit the sports teams to play up to seven games during the collegiate year, provided that the athletes maintained their class standings. The subcommittee also reminded the president that the athletic association had instituted a very effective "one-year rule" that eliminated a great many concerns.[53]

There is some evidence that Patterson knew in advance that he would not win this fight with the board. Whenever the trustees planned to take action on a hotly contested matter, Patterson frequently spent the preceding months campaigning for support among the individual trustees, prominent members of the faculty, alumni, and, if he thought it necessary, the governor. He often generated a tremendous volume of correspondence, which he carefully preserved with his other official papers. The lack of correspondence on this issue may well indicate that the outcome of the June meeting was not really in doubt. Indeed, Patterson offered no further arguments to the board. Sensing inevitable defeat, he responded simply by moving that the subcommittee's report be adopted.[54]

Across the nation, other college presidents met with a similar lack of success in their campaigns against collegiate football. Even schools that did ban the sport often saw it quickly reinstated. Harvard, for example, banned the sport three times.[55] Why were these presidents unable permanently to banish the sport from their campuses? Why did a game that many critics denounced prove so enduring at American colleges?

The game appeared on campuses at a time when many intellectuals began fearing a decline of virility because of growing urbanization and the loss of the frontier.[56] In 1881, Dr. George Beard sounded the alarm when he wrote that the new city brought with it new diseases of debility. These new forces drained the body of its nervous reserves and left it susceptible to a host of diseases. Beard concluded that "no age, no country, and no former civilization" had ever possessed such maladies.[57] These fears were only heightened when coupled with the concerns over the heavy volume of European immigration at that same time. Just as college football was making its debut on college campuses, many scholars were formulating the belief that these newcomers constituted backward races from inferior parts of Europe.[58] Eugenics advocate William Castle wrote that the greatest problem facing America was the dropping birthrate among the country's most valuable classes combined with the prolific increase in the "inferior classes." He claimed that one thousand Harvard men would produce only fifty descendants in two hundred years. Yet "one thousand Roumanians" would produce one hundred thousand offspring in the same period.[59] The nation's most visible football fan, Theodore Roosevelt, warned that no quality in a race could atone for the failure to produce an abundance of healthy children. If the nation lost its virile qualities, it would "reach a condition worse than that of ancient civilizations in the years of their decay."[60]

In view of such dark pronouncements, football served as a valuable symbol of manliness at the nation's finest colleges. Accordingly, a Brown University professor could state emphatically that national robustness through continued athletic exercise must be preserved to offset the weakness produced by city life and greater ease.[61] This sentiment echoed throughout Lexington. While denouncing the associated corruption, the *Herald* believed that football was the best training a young collegiate man could have. It noted that no weakling could play the game, nor could one succeed at it without developing self-control and courage.[62]

On a more practical note, the attempts by college presidents to ban football were often thwarted by their own bureaucracies. When trustees favored sports, it put the presidents in an awkward position because they were hired and fired by the trustees, and did not always wish to antagonize them. Even a president with exceptional institutional power such as Patterson could not always go against the wishes of the board. At the University of Kentucky, pro-sports administrators took great advantage of the slow decision-making process. UK trustees could drag their feet and appoint committees and subcommittees, thereby taking a great deal of wind out of Patterson's sails. The support of certain board members was not lost on the student body or the athletic association. The class of 1910 dedicated its yearbook to trustee Richard Stoll in part for his "enthusiasm in Athletic sports." When the university finally dedicated its football field, it bore the name Stoll Field.[63]

Presidents had to battle not only their own administrations but also town business leaders. In Lexington, football built up a feverish following. Merchants were especially strong in their support of the sport. Home games, especially the Thanksgiving game, brought thousands of spectators to town and thousands of dollars into the local economy. This situation was true on a much greater scale in larger cities such as New York or Chicago where tens of thousands of fans filled the giant stadiums.

Such defeats were not common for Patterson. He wielded considerable power at the university and generally received whatever he wanted from the faculty, trustees, and the legislature. The issue of athletics was a most notable defeat for him. He retired in 1910, never again calling for a ban on campus sports. In his last address to the board, one can see just how much he had resigned himself to the presence of athletics. In reviewing the events of the previous six months, he noted that the "season of field sports and athletic games" had been successful. He noted that he was pleased to report that the school had "in most instances led in the match games played and earned a reputation for themselves and for the university." Moreover, the teams had all "distinguished themselves for manliness and gentlemanliness, as well as for skill and endurance."[64]

3

A BRIEF MOMENT
IN THE SUN

*A good coach makes a good team and a good team is the best
advertisement an up-to-date school can have.*
                                        —UK student newspaper, 1909[1]

THE UNIVERSITY FOOTBALL PROGRAM may have escaped administrative sanction, but the future did not look promising. As was the case
a decade earlier, the team found itself beset by a host of difficulties
that threatened to destroy it. While the board ever so slowly debated
its future, the football team tried to schedule and play games. For
several years, however, it maintained only a very precarious existence
on the campus. Saddled by severe financial woes made even worse by
its inability to schedule a Thanksgiving game with Transylvania, the
whole program teetered on the brink of collapse.

A reprieve came when the team finally found a replacement for
Transylvania as the Thanksgiving Day opponent. In 1906, and especially from 1908 to 1910, thousands of fans packed the bleachers of
Stoll Field to witness the growing rivalry between the University of
Kentucky and Centre College. These games, and the revenue from
them, saved the university sports program and prepared the way for a
more modern athletic department in the next decade. In retrospect, it
is surprising not that the program attained the level of success that it
did (fourteen consecutive winning seasons) but that it survived these
lean and foreboding years at all.

Yet in 1906, the situation looked dismal. The *Herald* held out no
hope for continued football at either of the Lexington colleges. It reported in mid-September that unless drastic steps were taken, no team

would represent the Crimson of Transylvania and in all probability none would wear the Blue and White. The paper believed that only a successful Thanksgiving Day game could rescue the Kentucky teams. That one game could guarantee expenses for both colleges. Reports from the north end of Lexington, however, quickly dashed those hopes. The Transylvania board of curators announced that it had banned the sport for the year. Meanwhile, the UK team, still suffering the financial loss of the previous year's Thanksgiving fiasco, had neither a coach nor the funds to hire one.[2]

Such gloomy prospects quickly brightened on the UK campus. The football manager announced that he had persuaded 1905 team captain, Joel White Guyn, to coach. The yearbook euphemistically called this arrangement "the graduate system of coaching." In reality, Guyn (now the assistant city engineer) agreed to coach for no pay. He informed the *Herald* that the manager had booked several games and practice would begin shortly.[3] He scheduled only six games, yet critically, on October 10 he reported that he had at last been able to schedule a Thanksgiving game at home against a credible opponent, Centre College. After the debacles of the past few years, Lexington fans rejoiced at the opportunity to have another holiday game. The *Herald* also correctly noted that not only did the game serve as a sort of state championship, but the gate receipts could be counted on to "swell the athletic association's treasury."[4]

The path to the Thanksgiving game was not entirely smooth. The team opened with a very bad loss to Vanderbilt, followed by several close victories characterized by sloppy play. Nearly at the last minute, Berea canceled its game and the team had to scour the surrounding area for a replacement. The only available opponent came in the form of the little-known Eminence Athletic Club. The game was marred by the serious injury to starting UK guard, Harry Stevenson, who broke his leg in six places (originally diagnosed as two breaks). The injury occurred on the first scrimmage and sapped the spirit of the entire team. In typical fashion, the *Herald* dismissed the injury as highly unusual, noting that the Eminence player who tackled Stevenson was taking part in his first game, and in fact, his first tackle.[5]

An even stranger incident occurred in the next week's last-second victory over Kentucky Military Institute. In the second half, one of the grandstands "in which a large number of girls were sitting suddenly collapsed." Apart from a few bruises, no one sustained serious injury. A similar collapse had occurred the previous week in New York during the Syracuse-Colgate game. There, four hundred fans fell as the upper section of bleachers crumbled, injuring more than one hundred and killing three.[6]

Thanks in part to the demise of Transylvania and the poor showing of other local teams, the Thanksgiving game again shaped up as the state championship. The *Herald* proclaimed that once again Lexington had gone football mad. Not since 1903 had the interest and enthusiasm of Lexingtonians been more intense. Every street, hotel lobby, public place, and fireside rang with football discussions. The air also rang with the sound of hammers as the Lexington Lumber Company built new grandstands, each nine tiers high and 150 feet long.[7] The next day, 3,500 people filled the stands and watched Centre claim the championship.[8]

For the next two seasons, the redundant themes of financial hardship and squabbles with Transylvania plagued Guyn's team. In fact, both problems worsened during these years. The team found itself so short of money in 1907 that even as late as October 25, it was unable to supply all its players with suitable equipment.[9] Guyn had hoped to revive the training table used so successfully in 1903, but campus fundraisers generated only enough money for one meal. This supper "consisted mainly of such food as would strengthen the fibre of the men on the team." Inspired by the pep talks given by various speakers, several players promised not to smoke cigarettes, chew tobacco, or eat candy until the season ended.[10]

Once again, UK found it difficult to schedule reliable in-state opponents and played five out-of-state teams and three Kentucky foes. One of those games was a last-minute replacement game arranged with Manual Training High School of Louisville. As before, UK fared badly against the only major power it faced, losing 40-0 to Vanderbilt.[11] The team pinned its financial hopes on the Thanksgiving game with

Transylvania. The Crimson team made its reappearance, coached by 1903 star, Hogan Yancey. Crimson expectations remained low, but after a shocking 6-4 victory over Centre, Transylvania approached the Thanksgiving game undefeated.[12]

The sport could not escape the bitter hostility between the two schools, and for a while some fans feared the game would collapse under the weight of the latest argument. Two days before the game, the *Herald* reported that the University of Kentucky team threatened to go on strike. It claimed that Transylvania (the host of the game that year) had promised each player complimentary tickets. The UK athletic association demanded two tickets per player so that each could "give one to his sweetheart and one to his mother." The players claimed "that the presence of the lassies to cheer them on" would be "half of the victory." Transylvania refused to budge on this point, noting that its athletic association badly needed all the ticket money to defray current expenses.[13]

UK dropped its demands, and the town braced itself for what it hoped would be the greatest game of the season. Unfortunately for the townspeople and especially for the coffers of both teams, the weather did not cooperate. Game day brought with it heavy rains, and the teams feared that the weather would keep the crowd away from the Transylvania playing field. Both teams stated that they were anxious to play before a large crowd in order to recover the heavy expenses incurred over the course of the season. By mutual decree, they postponed the game until December 5.[14] They eventually met on that date, but only about half of the expected holiday crowd watched as UK defeated its crosstown rival by the score of 5-0 in a dull game.[15] This holiday disaster nearly paralyzed the UK team for the next year. When the 1908 season began, the athletic association could not outfit all of its players. The *Herald* noted that twelve men who wanted to try out for the team did not receive equipment. The team lacked the money to buy the suits, and these twelve aspirants "were thus held in check."[16]

The team manager devised several schemes to raise funds. He scheduled a game with the University of Michigan to be played in Ann Arbor in hopes of receiving a handsome appearance fee and a share of the gate receipts from Michigan's enormous crowd. Unfortunately, the high cost of travel ate up too much of the profits. The game also produced a humiliating 62-0 shutout.[17] The athletic association also urged Lexington merchants to join their ranks. In exchange for their dues, the businesses would receive season tickets and posters to display in their store windows proclaiming their support. The association hoped that UK students would boycott all nonmember merchants, but the plan failed miserably.[18]

The university was not alone in its fiscal hardship. Down the road at Winchester, the board of education at Kentucky Wesleyan College voted to ban football because of the team's inability to sustain itself financially. Local merchants presented a petition to the board hoping it would reverse itself. They believed that without athletics, the college attendance would drop sharply, draining a great deal of money that would otherwise be spent in town. The board softened its stand somewhat, prohibiting the team only from scheduling away games. In spite of this concession, the *Herald* pronounced sports dead in Winchester. The paper also described a great deal of dissension among the students.[19]

Many observers lamented that the athletic association had grown too dependent on a successful holiday game. They predicted that only a well-attended Thanksgiving game could save the UK team. The Lexingtonians who fervently hoped for a UK-Transylvania game received disappointing news in early November when the *Herald* announced that the two teams could not reach an agreement. The Kentucky manager next suggested that the schools play a December game as they had done the previous year. The Crimson manager bowed out, stating that the long season had been demoralizing and that extending it into December would disrupt classwork.[20]

To the delight of the Blue and White fans, the manager concluded successful negotiations with Centre for Thanksgiving. Soon the sound of construction filled the autumn air as once again the association built new bleachers at what was now being called Stoll Field. Starting a new trend, the association built fifteen private boxes (each seating six) and reserved them for trustees, news editors, the mayor, and the governor. The game exceeded all expectations. Not only did UK win 40-0, securing the state title, but the largest crowd in city history packed the newly constructed grandstands.[21]

The game propelled UK to success in intrastate competition for the next several years. The huge crowd provided the association coffers with enough money to buy new equipment and to secure the most precious of possessions—an "eastern" coach for the next season. In the fall of 1909, E.R. Sweetland arrived to coach the team. A collegiate All-American at Cornell, Sweetland had earlier coached at Ohio State, Syracuse, and Colgate. He would soon become the most beloved and arguably the best coach of the university's early years, posting a 23-5 record. Ultimately, he became the most controversial coach.[22] In addition to hiring a noted coach, the flush athletic association allowed UK to indulge in other luxuries. It scheduled eleven games, and throughout the entire 1909 season, the football team enjoyed a training table. The team also conducted the first spring practice at the university.[23]

The team ended the season with a 9-2 record. During the campaign, the Blue and White scored several notable victories. In early October, the team traveled north to take on the powerhouse University of Illinois. The players rode to the train station in a decorated wagon escorted by the school band, creating what the *Herald* described as a "considerable sensation."[24] An even greater sensation followed when UK defeated Illinois. That night, hundreds of students attired in nightshirts paraded through downtown Lexington.[25] Transylvania students and fans, however, did not share in this glee. They claimed that the victory was tainted because Illinois had held out several key players in order to have them fresh for their forthcoming game against the University of Chicago.[26]

Criticism from the north end of Lexington did not dampen the enthusiasm on the UK campus. In a rousing speech in chapel the next morning, Commandant Corbusier, who had traveled to the game, praised the team highly. He stated that even though its players were much smaller than their opponents (the backfield did not average more than 140 pounds), they had fought with the ferocity of mountain wildcats. The nickname became popular and quickly became the official team name.[27] The next week UK shut out Tennessee and later that season handed Transylvania a humiliating 77-0 defeat. This loss was symptomatic of Transylvania's steady decline. After defeating KMI in the first game, the Crimson went winless for the rest of the season. It failed to score, not only against Kentucky, but also against St. Mary's, Centre, Louisiana State, and Tennessee. After the LSU game, the Transylvania coach, Lee Coble, resigned and left town.[28]

The University of Kentucky claimed the state title by beating Centre 15-6 before six thousand fans who packed the rebuilt grandstands.[29] This level of success led many observers to think that UK had at last outgrown the KIAA. Indeed, the team's record for Sweetland's first year, combined with the previous five indicates that the Blue and White had posted a 27-1 record against Kentucky teams. The athletic association believed that it should look for new fields to conquer and began making plans to join the Southern Intercollegiate Athletic Association (SIAA), the forerunner of the Southeastern Conference. Supporters of the team thought that it had proved that it could "cope with the best of the Southern and Western teams." Such optimism may not have been entirely justified. Over the same six years just mentioned, UK won only eleven of twenty-one games against non-Kentucky teams.[30]

The only dark shadow across the successful season involved the health of Sweetland. In late October, the coach suddenly became ill. Many observers feared that he would not be able to resume his duties, and the student-manager began looking for a midseason replacement. Within a week, Sweetland had recovered enough to walk around, but the *Herald* claimed that he had decided to give up coaching.[31] The paper also reported that an ex-Cornell teammate of Sweetland had agreed to coach the team. This announcement proved premature as ten days later the soon-to-be Coach Parks was still attending Presbyterian Seminary in Pennsylvania. He finally arrived a few days before the Thanksgiving game.[32]

To the delight of UK fans, Sweetland recovered and took the helm again for spring practice and the 1910 season. In many regards, the season mirrored the previous one. Negotiations with Transylvania failed, the team played mostly non-Kentucky opponents and scored one notable upset—against the University of North Carolina. So many fans poured into Lexington to watch this game that the Carolina team had to travel all the way to Georgetown to find hotel vacancy. The victory also provoked another nightshirt parade.[33]

This continued success prompted many fans to dream of a permanent stadium. According to the *Herald,* many alumni favored constructing a concrete stadium modeled after that of Harvard. They claimed that the Thanksgiving game alone revealed the clear need of better facilities. A new stadium would also eliminate the recurring need to spend hundreds of dollars each season repairing and expanding the bleachers.[34] During the season, the students exhibited an increased interest in the game. For the first time, some of the university's "progressive supporters" arranged to have the highlights of the Tennessee game telegraphed from Knoxville to the Lexington campus. The student manager read the wired messages to the students assembled in the chapel. Between the reports, the band kept the audience entertained.[35]

The only departure from the previous year's experience came in the Thanksgiving clash with Centre. Although some spectators believed that the Wildcats played a "more brilliant game and made more and greater gains," it lost the game because of costly fumbles. UK finished the season with a 7-2 record, but Centre claimed the state championship honors.[36] Centre, however, did not play the role of the magnanimous victor. A brief verbal skirmish before the holiday game escalated, and the next day Centre announced that it had decided never to play the Wildcats again. In vague language, a college representative claimed that UK "had never acted fairly" in game negotiations (presumably by insisting that the game be played in Lexington). In sharper language, the Danville team stated that its players were so fearful of UK's actions that they carried their own food and water to Lexington. The Wildcat athletic association branded those allegations as childish, noting that the Centre team had dined at Lexington's Phoenix Hotel on a meal featuring tenderloin, rice, baked potatoes, and milk.[37]

The season was also marked by the retirement of one old nemesis and the reemergence of another. James K. Patterson announced his retirement after forty-one years as university president. Also, rumblings sounded from the KIAA and its most vocal administrator, A.H. Throckmorton. In November, Throckmorton announced that his diligent investigations had revealed that several of Centre's football players were not eligible to play. He claimed that the college had enrolled them knowing that their educational background was deficient and did not meet the minimum requirements established by the KIAA.[38] Shortly thereafter, he accused Centre of paying at least one of its athletes. Trying to claim a higher moral plane, Professor A.M. Miller of the UK athletic association condemned Centre, stating that the admission of students to a college without examination or even requiring certification from previous schools showed "to what lengths an institution may sometimes be forced by athletic pressure."[39]

The University of Kentucky football program did not escape Throckmorton's scrutiny. He indicated his sharp disapproval of the forthcoming UK-Centre game. In the holiday game, Centre played those team members that Throckmorton had declared ineligible. It did so, noting that both Centre and UK were also members of the SIAA, which had not ruled on the eligibility matter. Throckmorton replied that the new KIAA constitution prohibited members from joining any rival organization. Both Professor Miller and the *Herald* predicted that UK would withdraw from the KIAA. Such a move would of course prohibit them from playing other member institutions.[40]

Protected by sympathetic trustees, and sustained by the rabid enthusiasm of city residents, the University of Kentucky football team had risen to a position of prominence in the state. Indeed, at the end of the decade only UK and Centre had weathered the fiscal crises faced by so many Central Kentucky teams. It was clear to many observers that if the UK athletic association was to continue to grow, it would have to seek other opponents that would be more reliable and profitable than those scheduled in the past. The threats emanating from Throckmorton and the KIAA only added urgency to the matter.

Unfortunately at such an unsettled time, Sweetland's health again failed. This time, he did indeed submit his resignation, indicating that he was considering the less stressful position of rowing coach at the University of Wisconsin.[41] The students were outraged. Ignoring the matter of Sweetland's health, they claimed that his resignation stemmed from the unwillingness of the school to pay a better salary. The student newspaper, the *Idea*, claimed that he had coached at other universities for double his current salary. Whatever the reason, "the man who shaped the destiny of Kentucky's team" was gone, leaving it to face uncertain times.[42]

A SHELTER
FROM THE STORM

THE BARKER YEARS

As President of State University, I desire to express my appre-
ciation of the magnificent efforts of the football team, not only to
play successful games and win victories, but to play manly and
generous football.

—UK President Henry S. Barker[1]

SOME OF THE UNCERTAINTY surrounding the university sports program dissipated when the board of trustees nominated fellow board
member Henry Stites Barker to succeed Patterson as UK president.
As a trustee, Barker had been very sympathetic to the college athletic
program. Patterson opposed this nomination fiercely. He believed that
a university president should hold a doctorate degree and have publications, as well as knowledge of several foreign languages. Accordingly, he objected to Judge Barker's candidacy, writing that Barker
lacked "the indispensable condition of university training, experience,
and scholarship." Patterson went as far as to ask the board "to strike
out from the report of the [nominating] committee the name of Judge
H.S. Barker." He then made a motion that the name of his longtime
friend E.B. Smith, president of Tulane University, be inserted in place
of Barker. No one seconded the motion, and the board approved Barker
by a 12-0 vote, with Patterson abstaining.[2]

Although Patterson could not prevent Barker's hiring, he
was successful in delaying it. His resignation became effective
January 10, 1910, yet Patterson held onto the presidency, claiming
that Barker needed more training before assuming the full responsi-

bilities of the office. In May, Patterson did ask to be relieved of some administrative duties, but he requested that the help come from James White, then vice-president. The board later made White acting president, giving the university for a brief time an odd combination of a president emeritus, an acting president, and a president-elect.[3] The relationship between Patterson and Barker quickly became bitter. Patterson, reveling in his role as president emeritus, refused to vacate the president's mansion, forcing Barker and his wife to live in a remodeled dormitory apartment. Barker, in return, suspended Patterson's pension and spent the rest of his presidency trying to evict him from his campus residence. This particular conflict continued for years, yielding only to a decision (in Patterson's favor) made by the state attorney general in 1918.[4]

Barker quickly proved to be a very different president than Patterson had been. He delegated a great deal of authority, preferred to have the students discipline themselves with a new honor system, and winked at some student activities that would have enraged his predecessor. He also expressed a very different attitude concerning college athletics. Unlike Patterson, Barker not only was a sports fan himself but he believed that college athletics could be a positive force for good. Specifically, he thought that sports served as excellent advertising for the university throughout the state and attracted students to the school. He also thought that a successful sports program elicited financial support from the alumni.[5]

In an editorial printed in the student newspaper, Barker wrote that the entire university owed a debt of gratitude to the football team members who by their courage, endurance, patience, and self-sacrifice had earned a fine reputation for the university throughout the region. He continued, noting that college sports served a valuable role "as an adjunct of the student body." Anyone associated with the program had "great cause to congratulate themselves on the outlook which athletics presents today on the campus."[6]

The Barker family became a fixture in its private box at Stoll Field. Additionally, the president could always be counted on for a rousing speech at the many pep rallies held during morning chapel. The stu-

President Henry S. Barker

dents were especially fond of his reminiscences about "football in the days of yore."[7]

The football team presented the new president with several opportunities to show both his support and especially his tolerance. During a midseason game against the University of Cincinnati, for example, a UK player started a fight with a UC lineman. The referee attempted to eject him, but the angry Wildcat turned his wrath upon the official, knocking him down and cutting his lip severely with punches to the face. Barker issued a personal apology to the referee, stating that he "would rather have lost an hundred football games than have had this happen."[8]

Most UK fans expected the athletic association to ban the offending player from any further games. In an unusual move, Barker decided to allow the bruised official to rule on the matter. Referee W.C. Knight replied that he believed that the Wildcat in question should be permitted to play. Knight reasoned that "for such a man, the game of football would be good training." He hoped that the discipline of the game would teach him to control his temper.[9]

Two weeks later, Barker had an even more spectacular opportunity to test his tolerance of football-inspired mischief. During the November 10 game, Transylvania scored twelve points late in the fourth quarter and, to the shock of many, defeated the Wildcats. It was the Tigers' (Transylvania's new and short-lived nickname) first victory over their archrival since the famous 1903 Ringer Game. Indeed, it was the first time since 1904 that Transylvania had scored at all against UK.[10] The stunning upset provoked a spirited response from Tiger fans. That night, Transylvania supporters dressed in nightshirts and carrying clubs marched down Main Street, running headlong into a large UK contingent. Violence seemed imminent, and the police appeared powerless to stop it. As the UK student newspaper described, "just at the critical moment," President Barker waded into the thickest part of the mob "and commanded the paraders to march on."[11]

Aside from the loss to Transylvania, the 1911 season raised few eyebrows. In fact, the student body proved to be curiously critical of a team that posted a 7-3 record. For starters, the student newspaper appeared unhappy with the choice of P.P. Douglass (a graduate of the University of Michigan) and 1910 captain Richard S. Webb, Jr., as coaches. It had hoped the team would hire an established coach to fill the shoes of the much-lamented Sweetland. The paper blamed this lack of a noted coach on student apathy. In a September editorial, the *Idea* criticized the UK students for not supporting the team financially. It stated that out of the one thousand students, only three hundred had bought season tickets. The days were long passed, it noted, when a good coach could "be gotten for an insignificant sum." The paper urged all students to buy at least one (or more) of the tickets.[12]

The *Herald* also criticized the performance of the team, even in victory. According to the paper, the shutout victories over Maryville and Morris-Harvey demonstrated the team's weak backfield and poor line. It described the Wildcats as being very much outclassed by the University of Cincinnati and especially by Vanderbilt. In general, it appeared that football throughout the state was flat. Centre had a terrible time scheduling games. Its first three opponents canceled with little notice, and it was almost November before it fielded a team. In Winchester, the Kentucky Wesleyan College board of education once again banned athletics. Transylvania repeatedly claimed that poor officiating robbed it of victory. One argument with the referee became so heated that the Transylvania team walked off the field, forfeiting their game with Morris-Harvey. The *Herald* declared the state championship to be a stale three-way tie.[13]

Despite the angry words of the previous year, the UK athletic association was able to schedule a game with Centre—but not for Thanksgiving. Centre chose instead to play Transylvania in the holiday game. Some observers feared this arrangement would cripple the Wildcats financially. Such concerns were, however, unfounded, and the team succeeded in scheduling the University of Tennessee for the season finale. Thirty-five hundred fans filled the Stoll Field bleachers to watch the home team win what the *Idea* described as only an average game.[14] If this first UK-UT holiday game did not live up to everyone's expectations, the series quickly became popular, and throughout the period (continuing to the present) the game marked the end of the season.[15]

If the 1911 season had been dull, the events of the next year certainly reversed the trend. That spring, the administration, at Barker's behest, took action that would shape athletics at the university for years to come. Barker believed that previously (under Patterson), the administration had interfered too much with athletics. To that end, he abolished the governing body of the athletic association, the faculty athletic committee. In its place, Barker created the position of athletic director with faculty status and the same "prestige and responsibility of any department chair." The athletic director and a ten-member board composed of five professors, two students, and three alumni formed an athletic council that made all decisions concerning sports. The university president served as an ex officio member of the council.[16]

Most critically, the board gave the athletic director and his assistant coaches faculty salaries. Never again would the football team begin a season without a coach because of a lack of funds. This action was of immense importance for the so-called minor sports; the assistant football coaches also served as coaches for sports such as track and men's and women's basketball. The board also placed the men's and women's departments of physical education under the control of the athletic department. Additionally, the finances of sports and physical education were combined. Barker sincerely hoped that the new department would be self-sustaining financially and would not become a drain on university coffers. One of the department's first actions did indeed cut some of its operating costs. In August, it trimmed one of its largest expenses by lowering the salaries of the men's and women's physical education instructors by 20 percent.[17]

The announcement that the board had persuaded E.R. Sweetland to fill the new position of athletic director swept through the student body. The lead athletic story in the 1912 yearbook was not the 1911 team's 7-3 record. It was instead the news of Sweetland's return. In stirring rhetoric, the *Kentuckian* proclaimed, "Yes, he has come back—the courteous gentleman, the true sportsman, the loyal friend." Dick Webb continued on as assistant football coach and also served as the assistant athletic director.[18]

Sweetland had little time to relish his hearty welcome. Throughout the spring, the rumor persisted that the KIAA planned to take harsh disciplinary action against the university. He at first attempted to steal some of the KIAA's thunder by declaring that the university had long since outgrown the league. On May 28, the *Herald* reported that Sweetland planned formally to withdraw the school from the KIAA at the end of the baseball season. Sweetland noted that the Wildcats had won more state titles than all the other member schools and that while UK had grown steadily stronger, the other member schools had noticeably weakened. UK would try to schedule more SIAA teams or at least more competitive ones.[19] A week later the KIAA reported that based upon its investigation of the UK sports program, it was suspending the university for one year because of various rules violations. It accused the school of playing ineligible athletes and, in the case of baseball, allowing professionals to play. It ordered the baseball team to forfeit its state title and banned UK from playing any member school in any sport for the next year.[20]

Athletic director E.R. Sweetland poses in front of his undefeated 1912 basketball team.

Sweetland tried to dismiss the rebuke of the league as insignificant, but the one-year ban loomed ominous. Finding opponents that were not KIAA members would be difficult, especially when Centre indicated that it would remain in the league. Many Wildcat fans feared the ban would jeopardize a Thanksgiving game with Centre or Transylvania, wrecking the team's finances.[21] After a great deal of hustling, Sweetland succeeded in filling the schedule for the 1912 season. He did so by arranging games with teams from Ohio, West Virginia, Virginia, and Tennessee. Yet negotiations for a Thanksgiving game with a noted rival such as Transylvania, Centre, or Tennessee failed, and instead, Sweetland settled for a holiday bout with the Cincinnati YMCA.

A number of unfolding events that fall marred Sweetland's homecoming. Throughout much of October, the rumor lingered that the

F. Paul Anderson,
dean of engineering

KIAA had leaked the findings of its investigation of the university to the SIAA. The situation worsened in late October when the athletic council, after reviewing its own records, suspended a player, claiming that he was ineligible. Another rumor then leaked out that more suspensions were forthcoming. Such a possibility resulted in growing animosity between the students and the administration. The *Herald* reported that "some of the more radical of the students" had singled out one prominent council member, Paul Anderson, dean of the engineering school as being unduly harsh on matters of athletic eligibility.[22]

This animosity steadily escalated. Posters on campus bearing the messages "To Hell with Little Paul!" or "Benedict Arnold lies in a traitor's grave but little Paul still lives" boded ill. So too did the bullet holes in the window screens on Anderson's office windows.[23] The week before the much anticipated game with Virginia Military Institute, the council announced the suspension of star quarterback Jim Park, pending further investigation of his eligibility. The previous year the KIAA had declared him ineligible on charges of professionalism, but as yet the SIAA had made no ruling.[24]

News of the suspension caused an even greater uproar on the campus. Shortly after the announcement, a fire broke out in Anderson's office in Mechanical Hall. The fire caused little damage to the building, but it destroyed the contents of the office. Those items included several of Anderson's personal belongings and several important university records. Chief among these documents, as reported at the time, were the eligibility records of football team members. Both the student newspaper and the *Herald* originally reported that "crossed electrical wires" had started the fire. After a more careful investigation, however, the official ruling pointed to arson.

The discovery of several of Anderson's personal effects added credence to this verdict. A few days after the fire, several young boys who generally played near the football practice field found some unusual items. They reported their discovery to assistant coach Dick Webb, who at one time had worked in the Mechanical Building. Webb identified the objects as several cut glass bowls and a slide rule belonging to Anderson. The authorities quickly deduced that the office had been robbed shortly before the fire because all of the other contents of the office had been thoroughly destroyed or at least greatly damaged by the blaze.[25]

For some onlookers, most notably Patterson, the link between the fire and the football team looked incriminating. President Barker at first tried to gloss over the episode, reminding the board that the insurance companies covered the $3,100 in damages. He also noted that the whole matter was in the hands of the proper authorities, where it should be left. The board, on the other hand, reacted a bit more forcefully. It passed a resolution stating that it very much regretted "the unfortunate developments in the athletic situation at the University." It urged the president and the executive committee to take prompt action in investigating the cause of the fire and any link with "the athletic disturbances."[26]

While these rumors circulated, more bad news flooded in. In

James Park, football quarterback and baseball pitcher

late November, the SIAA suspended the university athletic program for an unspecified period. The SIAA charges mirrored those brought by the KIAA earlier that spring. Specifically, the southern league declared quarterback Jim Park ineligible because he had played baseball for pay in a summer league. The SIAA also penalized UK for admitting some football players without sufficient entrance credits and claimed that the Wildcat baseball team had violated the one-year rule.

To these charges the SIAA added one that had not been made previously by the KIAA. The new charge centered on the football team's star halfback, "Doc" Rodes. He had skipped spring and preseason practice but showed up unexpectedly the day of the October 6 Marshall game and singlehandedly (the *Herald* thought) won the game. According to the SIAA, however, he would have done well to have stayed away. The organization's executive committee ruled that he had played longer than the four years allowed by league rules.[27]

Five days after this announcement, the Wildcats closed the disastrous season with a dull Thanksgiving game against the underpowered YMCA team from Cincinnati. In hopes of boosting attendance, the athletic department had scheduled a holiday doubleheader for Stoll Field. Spectators at the first game saw Lexington High School defeat the UK freshmen by the score of 14-0. A late-arriving crowd of 2,500 watched as the varsity routed the hapless YMCA team, 56-0.[28]

After the close of the season, bad news for the athletic department came in torrents. In mid-December, the state fire marshall investigating the campus arson became troubled by the contradictory testimony he had compiled. It seemed to him that the statements made by the now-former assistant football coach, Dick Webb, clashed with all others he had taken. Webb had stated that he left campus after eating supper at the football team's training table at 6:45 and returned to the home of his parents in downtown Lexington. Numerous other witnesses, however, had reported that they had seen Webb on campus between 9 and 11 o'clock that evening.[29]

The fire marshall, police chief, and district attorney believed that this contradiction cast enough suspicion upon Webb to merit bringing charges against him at least for perjury and perhaps for arson. This was not a decision they made hastily. Webb was an extremely popular figure in town. He had been captain of the football team in 1910, selected for All-Kentucky honors, and "tipped by men who knew football as the best center in the south." He also belonged to a very prominent Lexington family. Moreover, in addition to his coaching position, he served as an officer of the court. Specifically, at the time of his arrest he was the assistant probation officer.[30]

The ensuing trial caused a great stir in Lexington. In the words of the *Herald,* no case had attracted such interest owing to the "prominence of the principals" and the connection with UK football. Many legal experts believed that securing an indictment against such a popular person from such a notable family would prove to be a formidable task for the prosecution. The task grew even more daunting when the Webb family assembled a team of the finest attorneys in all the Bluegrass. Among them were Judge George C. Webb (no relation), Judge Samuel M. Wilson, and the renowned Henry S. Breckinridge.

The preliminary examination began January 3, lasted a week, and saw fifty witnesses called. During this period, spectators packed the courtroom, occupying every seat, bench, and standing space. So great was the crush of onlookers that the judge moved the proceeding to a larger courtroom. Even so, the crowd spilled out into the hallway. The prose- cution's case hinged upon two tactics. It first hoped to show that the relation between Webb and head coach Sweetland had deteriorated sharply, as had that between Webb and Professor Anderson. To that end district attorney J.A. Edge called several UK administration figures as witnesses. President Barker testified that Webb and Sweetland had at one time been close friends. In fact, Webb had convinced Barker to rehire Sweetland in 1911, calling him "the greatest coach living." He also testified that Webb had petitioned him to oust Anderson from the faculty athletic committee because of the Park incident.

Edge next called Anderson, who noted that Sweetland had asked him to retain Webb as assistant coach. He also stated that the relation between the men had at first been close. But he further testified that Sweetland had fired Webb late in the 1912 season. According to Anderson and Professor A.M. Miller, Sweetland had fired Webb after dis-

*Richard S. Webb, football
coach and arson suspect*

covering that the assistant coach had taken the team on a tour of Knoxville's bawdy district following the game with the University of Tennessee.[31] The court also heard from W. C. Wilson, a UK student, who testified that he had overheard Webb threaten to "put holes in Sweetland" after the coach had fired him.[32]

Prosecutor Edge's second strategy involved testimony from several UK students who swore that they had seen Webb on the campus shortly before the fire alarm sounded. The most damaging testimony came from football team member Ellis Hayden. He stated under oath that Webb had come to his room between 9:00 and 11:00 on the night of the fire. When asked the purpose of his visit, Webb reportedly told Hayden that he was there "to raise a stink." His testimony was corroborated by roommate Floyd Galloway. On cross-examination, Breckinridge quizzed the students concerning when they had actually seen Webb. Despite their testimony to the contrary, the defense tried to establish that the students were mistaken as to the date. He referred to them as "deluded individuals who fancied themselves to have seen the defendant at incriminating times."[33]

The defense team followed a twofold plan of its own. First, it tried to supply an alibi for Webb. To that end it called several of his relatives, including his aunt, sister, and father, who testified that Webb had been at home from 8:00 P.M. until the next morning.[34] Second, Webb took the stand and affirmed that he had been at home during the evening in question. He noted that Hayden and Galloway were mistaken about which day he had visited them. According to Webb, the visit occurred the night before the fire. He also tried to blunt prosecution testimony by claiming that he was fired from the football team because of a lack of funds and had never petitioned Barker for Anderson's removal. Next, he tried to direct suspicion toward Sweetland, who, according to Webb, was mentally unstable.

The prosecution made great haste to poke holes in Webb's allegations. It re-called several witnesses to testify to Sweetland's state of mind. Barker first stated that he had never seen any examples of mental instability. He did note, however, that it was common knowledge that Sweetland had once suffered a severe concussion and that he disliked riding trains or climbing above the second floor in buildings, as these actions brought on headaches.[35] Edge then re-called Professor Anderson, who testified that contrary to the three-month-old rumor, his office had not housed athletic records on the eve of the fire. Anderson stated that he had returned all such records as well as team funds to Sweetland long before the fire. On cross-examination, Breckinridge asked if he thought that Sweetland was crazy. The courtroom then exploded in objections and arguments. When order was restored, Anderson answered that Sweetland at times appeared nervous but not unstable. Professor Miller gave similar testimony.[36]

The next day the prosecution held its breath and called Sweetland to the stand. He testified that he had never done anything that would make people think he was crazy. The thirty-eight-year-old coach stated that he did not drink alcohol and denied defense allegations that he had ever undergone brain or skull surgery. He did indicate that he appeared nervous at times but that this was a common ailment in his profession.[37] He further stated that his friendship with Webb had begun to deteriorate when the two men jointly purchased some property near the UK campus. During Sweetland's absence, the house on the lot burned down, and Webb then sold the property for a handsome profit to the university, which was planning to expand in that direction. Sweetland testified that it had been his intention to remodel the house and live in it—not to fleece the school. The two argued over the sale of the property, the division of the money, and the nature of the fire, which Sweetland believed to be suspicious. Sweetland also described the events that led to his discharging Webb. Here he corroborated Anderson's testimony about the Knoxville red-light district episode. On cross-examination, the defense asked numerous questions concerning Sweetland's sanity, all of which were objected to by the prosecution and sustained by the judge.[38]

In its closing statement, the defense argued that the prosecution had not presented "a single syllable of evidence" against Webb. It had, Breckinridge claimed, failed in demonstrating that Webb could have possibly had a motive for the crime. Breckinridge believed that suspicion pointed directly or indirectly to Sweetland. "I am not prepared to say," he told the court, "that Sweetland applied the match, but I do hold him responsible." As Breckinridge explained, Sweetland was a very influential person on campus. Yet not once did he use his influence to quell the tide of opposition to Anderson. The defense counsel also told the court that he had tired of the prosecution's "sinister hints" that it had a mystery witness that saw Webb commit the crime. He challenged the district attorney either to produce the witness or apologize to the court.

Edge concluded his case by briefly restating the key prosecution points. He reminded the court that half a dozen witnesses placed Webb at the scene. He also reviewed Webb's growing animosity toward Sweetland and Anderson, which he claimed provided a clear motive. Webb set the fire, Edge concluded, in order to discredit Anderson and Sweetland. Perhaps Webb had believed that by doing so, he could regain his former position as head coach. Both sides rested and awaited the decision of the court.[39] The prosecution won this first round, and as reported by the *Herald* on January 11, the judge ruled that probable cause existed to hold Webb on the charge of arson.[40]

During the interval between the preliminary examination and the grand jury indictment, the prosecution at long last located its mystery witness. With the help of the Ohio police (and a total disregard for extradition procedures), assistant fire marshall J.J. Peel arrested and brought former UK student and Harrison County native Thomas Butler back to Lexington on January 12. Butler subsequently pleaded guilty to the campus arson and indicated that Webb had been his accomplice. His statement was very damaging and also strengthened that of UK student Paul Gerhardt who had previously testified that he had seen Webb and Butler together on campus shortly before the fire alarm sounded.[41]

The prosecution, as well as the UK administration, hoped for a speedy trial date to lay the matter to rest. They received their wish, and the case was placed on the spring docket as the last case tried in Lexington during that session. In the meantime, a few related events transpired. First, Webb resigned his post as probation officer, indicating that he did not want any suspicion of wrongdoing to impair his ability to execute the duties of his office. Second, the UK athletic department announced that Coach Sweetland "could not be induced to stay." Although he announced that he had no immediate plans, Sweetland soon accepted the head coaching position at the University of West Virginia.[42]

The April trial, although shorter than the preliminary trial, still caused a great commotion in the city. Both opposing counsels spent the better part of the trial's first day issuing their opening statements to the jury. The prosecution told the jury that it would prove that Dick Webb had "entertained a resentment" toward Professor Anderson and Coach Sweetland. Accordingly, Webb set the fire in hopes of discrediting both men. In turn, the district attorney noted, Webb hoped that Sweetland would resign in disgrace, leaving the head coaching position open for him to fill. It also claimed to have fingerprint evidence linking Webb to the crime scene. After the preliminary trial, the defense dropped its tactic of directing blame to Sweetland by painting him as unstable. Instead it opened its remarks by emphasizing its key points. First it noted that the defendant came from a prominent Lexington family of unimpeachable character. Several family members would, in the course of the trial, testify that Dick Webb had been at home during the night in question. Second, the defense pointed out, most of the prosecution's evidence was merely circumstantial in nature and thus unreliable. The defense also labeled the alleged fingerprint evidence as unreliable. It told the jury that such evidence was experimental and had never been admitted into evidence in a Fayette County court. Finally, the defense began its long campaign to discredit the testimony of Thomas Butler. In a sea of potentially irrelevant circumstantial evidence, Butler was the only real eyewitness. Whom should they believe, the defense asked the jury, a respectable Lexington family or a confessed felon? At the end of the first day, the *Herald* believed that the prosecution had presented the stronger case. As the paper described, the combination of circumstantial, fingerprint, and eyewitness evidence would prove quite damning.[43]

The next day, Lexingtonians packed the courtroom, eager to hear the prosecution's star witness, Thomas Butler. He stated that he and Webb walked to the Mechanical Building on the night of October 30. Once there, he tore off the screens to the second-floor window and climbed into Anderson's office. Butler then threw to Webb (who remained outside) several items from the office. At that time, "nothing had been said about setting fire to the office." Webb and Butler next carried their plunder to the athletic field and other spots around campus.

Butler indicated that the pair made a second trip to Anderson's office, this time with a revised plan. According to his testimony, they decided to start a small fire that would attract a crowd of students. Webb climbed into the office and handed several more items to Butler, who hid them "in the old smokestack." Webb then set fire to the office. Butler testified that the two had discussed starting a fire in the office wastepaper basket, but he admitted that he was outside when the fire began and did not actually see Webb strike the match. The two men then walked to the Agriculture Building and sat down on the steps to watch.[44] The defense did very little to attack the contents of Butler's confession. Webb's attorneys instead tried to cast doubts on his motives. Yet on cross-examination, Butler steadfastly denied that he had struck a deal for clemency or leniency in exchange for his testimony.[45]

Butler's testimony was, according to the *Herald*, very convincing. Undaunted, the defense team scored several major victories close on the heels of this setback. In the absence of the jury, both sides discussed at length the admissibility of several key items of the prosecution's evidence. First, the opposing counsels debated the admissibility of the fingerprint evidence. The defense launched a withering attack on the prosecution's fingerprint expert, Ray Campbell of the Indiana State Reformatory. In testimony not heard by the jury, he admitted that "he knew practically nothing of the various authors and textbooks on the subject, except one publication by a Chicago detective concern." Upon a defense motion, the judge excluded the expert's testimony and all fingerprint evidence as incompetent.[46]

The defense next questioned the admissibility of some damaging testimony. Prior to the arrest of Webb, the fire marshall and the police had questioned him at length. During this time, he made some damaging statements that led to his arrest and trial. The defense moved that this evidence should be excluded because the defendant had been "brought before the inquisitorial body under a subpoena and not admonished that he was not required to answer any questions that might incriminate himself." Much to the bitter disappointment of the prosecution, the judge concurred.[47]

The prosecution suffered another defeat when it tried to introduce an anonymous letter into evidence. The letter, written to Butler in jail, repeatedly urged him to renounce his confession and plead not guilty. The judge ruled the letter irrelevant and incompetent. This third loss angered the prosecution immensely, and a heated argument broke out among the attorneys. It took the judge several minutes to restore order, at which time he cited both sides for contempt and fined them two dollars apiece for what he euphemistically termed "indulging in personal compliments" and delaying the trial.[48]

With much of its key evidence excluded, the prosecution called its last witnesses. The court then heard from four UK students who testified that they had seen Webb on the college grounds the night of the fire. The *Herald* thought that the most damaging blows came from Ellis Hayden, who restated his earlier testimony that Webb had come to his dorm room that night saying that "he was going to raise a stink." Two hours later, the fire alarm sounded. After this testimony, the prosecution rested and court adjourned for the day.[49]

During the trial's fourth day, the defense team made a strong attempt to establish an alibi for Webb. During the morning session, the jury listened as Webb's mother, father, sister, aunt, and "venerable grandfather" all confirmed that Webb had been at home the night of the fire from eight o'clock that evening until the next morning and never at any time left the house. The defendant then took the stand for what appeared to many observers to be four hours of uneventful testimony. Webb stated that he never harbored any animosity toward Anderson or Sweetland, nor did he ever sign a petition to have Anderson removed from the athletic board.

Closing arguments on the trial's fifth and final day brought an end to "the most notable case on record in the Fayette Circuit Court." Standing room in the court was at a premium, and the overflow crowd extended far out into the corridors. The defense argued that the prosecution had failed to prove that Webb had a motive for burning Anderson's office. It claimed that Adams had not proved that Webb wanted "to even up matters with Anderson" or "to cast suspicion on Sweetland and thereby get rid of him." The very idea that the defendant hoped to replace Sweetland as head coach was ridiculous and nothing more than vicious gossip.

The defense team focused most of its closing statement on the character of the prosecution's star witness. It described Butler as "a pitiable object, an outcast, a fugitive, a perjurer, and a self-confessed felon." Yet, of all of Butler's crimes, his most serious offense was implicating the innocent Webb. The defense concluded its address by asking the jury whether they would believe the wayward Butler or "a man of good reputation and a family worthy of respect and belief."[50]

In its closing statement, the prosecution tried to negate the strategy of the defense. Adams openly acknowledged the influence of the Webb family. He conceded that the high character of the family had indeed made the trial a painful duty for the prosecution, but, he quickly added, the enforcement of the law was paramount. He told the jury that it might indeed seem strange to see a young man from such a fine family on trial, but the evidence clearly indicated his guilt. In conclusion, he stated that "we have little trouble in convicting a Negro in this court, or a white man without influence." But his experience had taught him "that when a man of influence has committed a crime, no matter how revolting, sentiment plays a prominent part." But in this case, the jury could not hide behind sentiment. It had to decide the case fairly, based upon cold facts.[51]

The *Herald* wrote that the prosecution had presented a powerful and brilliant summation.[52] The jury, however, did not seem to concur. It received the case at 9:30 Saturday morning and at 10:15 returned a verdict of not guilty. Webb returned to the bosom of his family, and Butler went to the penitentiary. The *Herald,* although greatly surprised, offered no editorial on the verdict. The UK student newspaper also sidestepped the issue of Webb's guilt or innocence, but stated that it admired "the manhood of Butler who made a complete confession and paid the penalty for his rash act."[53]

President Barker was more than happy to sweep the remains of this incident under the rug. While declining to comment "upon the merits of the acquittal," he finally conceded that the trouble had grown out of a disagreement between the head football coach and his assistant. He tried to solace the board with the knowledge that both Webb and Sweetland had severed all ties with the university. As only he would, Barker tried to put a positive spin on the scandal, noting that the trial had clearly demonstrated that the student body had nothing whatsoever to do with the crime. He told the board that the incident offered proof of the high moral fiber and loyalty of the students. He believed that the students had actually benefited from the occurrence. According to Barker, they had been sobered by the unjust suspicion that they were participants in the crime. Finally, he thought that the unfortunate matter had generated "a better college spirit than we had before."[54]

In the aftermath of the trial, the athletic department had to hope that its supporters believed Barker's rosy assessment that everything was "behind us now."[55] It also had to replace personnel. It accomplished part of that task with an internal transfer. Professor J.J. Tigert, chair of philosophy, filled the vacant athletic director's spot. Tigert had been a four-sports star at Vanderbilt, captaining the football and basketball teams. He was a unanimous choice as an All-Southern running back and had won acclaim at Oxford University for his rowing. After graduating from Oxford, Tigert secured employment at Central College in Missouri, where he taught philosophy and coached football. In 1908, he left Missouri and became president of Kentucky Wesleyan College. After two years in Winchester, he migrated to UK. At various times, he coached the running backs, the freshmen football team, and basketball.[56]

Early in the fall, the athletic department filled its other key vacancy by hiring Alpha Brummage, formerly of Virginia Military Institute, as head football coach. Brummage soon took over the athletic director's responsibilities (as well as coaching men's basketball and baseball), allowing Tigert more time to devote to his academic duties. The department also filed a successful appeal with the SIAA to reinstate the eligibility of quarterback Jim Park.[57]

Brummage did not stay long, submitting his resignation at the end of the 1914 season. Unlike some of his predecessors, who left to coach elsewhere, Brummage announced that he was retiring from the profession. Many fans lamented this decision, noting his 11-5 record at UK, and his career winning percentage that topped .700.[58] Professor Tigert again stepped in to fill this vacancy. His twin responsibilities as athletic director and head coach proved to be extremely demanding. To that end, he took a leave of absence from the classroom. His salary for the next two years came out of the athletic coffers.[59] The year 1914 also marked the last football season for Jim Park, who left the Bluegrass for professional baseball. He took with him an enduring team record. In the 1914 game against Earlham College, Park passed for five touchdowns and ran for five more scores.[60] As 1915 arrived, it appeared as if the program had at last escaped the strain of the 1912 scandal. Barker's protection saved the program from immediate sanction, while the football team's continued success and Tigert's very clean and scholarly image restored the faith of many UK supporters. Once again, the UK faithful renewed their hopes for a new, permanent stadium for Stoll Field. In 1914, the *Leader* revived the old rumor that the university would build a new facility on land near the campus that had been used as a dump. In October, the paper reported that the university had purchased the ten-acre tract from the city. The student newspaper, the *Idea,* disapproved of this plan, noting that future construction plans called for a concrete stadium. Such a structure could not be built upon the rather unstable ground of the dump. The student newspaper believed that the more logical solution would be to expand the present playing field further to the west.[61]

When the 1915 season began, Stoll Field contained three new fields. The new practice fields had been laid out east of the stadium while a new gridiron at the west end was reserved only for games. The coaches greatly welcomed the additional practice area as an ideal solution to this chronic lack of space. As the *Herald* described, now men would not run all over each other during workouts. Reserving one field for games would allow the grass to stay green and beautiful all season. Although hopes for a new concrete stadium did not materialize, the athletic department did build new bleachers along both sides of the new field.[62]

Popular opinion proclaimed the new field beautiful and the finest in the South.[63] The only difficulty centered on what to call the newly designed complex. Originally the athletic authorities had decided to name it Barker Stadium in honor of the university president. Many people, however, favored retaining the old title of Stoll Field. Among them was Barker himself, who believed that it would be "in keeping with the tender memories connected with the university athletic field to retain the old name."[64]

These improvements proved to be a mixed blessing. Although widely acclaimed, they also devastated the athletic budget. In early 1917, the *Leader* reported that the program was so deeply in debt that it might discontinue intercollegiate sports for the remainder of the year. At a meeting in his office, Barker explained to various student representatives and the city media that the expansion of Stoll Field had resulted in a debt approaching four thousand dollars. Football revenues had been counted on to pay for this project but had fallen short. As Barker explained, the Tennessee and Vanderbilt games had netted about two thousand dollars, but the other games had been played at a loss. Complicating matters, "friends of the university had given their personal notes for financing the improvements." These notes were about to fall due. Barker stated that unless drastic action were taken soon, athletics "would have to be temporarily abandoned." The students quickly responded by voting for a $2.50 raise in the student fee. The fee had previously been $15, of which $5 had gone to athletics. The increase produced approximately $2,500, which bailed out the spring sports, including basketball, baseball, and track. Barker assured the *Leader* that the decision to raise the student fee was voluntary and entirely a student question.[65]

Athletics prospered during the Barker administration. Unfortunately, his term came to a rather unexpected end. His downfall began in January 1917 when the governor appointed a review committee to study Barker's proposed merger of the university's engineering schools. The governor also charged the committee with the responsibility of conducting interviews, sending out questionnaires, and making recommendations concerning the operation of the university as a whole. In all, the committee made sixty-nine recommendations. Although it did endorse Barker's consolidation program, it voiced sharp criticisms of Barker. As it described, the university suffered from the lack of an adequate conception of the presidency. The committee believed that the university should be headed by an educational expert thoroughly experienced in university administration. Barker, the committee added, was not such an expert. It compared him to a ship's captain who had never studied navigation. In conclusion, the review committee proclaimed that the welfare of the school demanded Barker's early retirement. It cited September 1918 as a target date. In June, the UK board of trustees accepted nearly all of the committee's recommendations. Barker, stung by the board's decision, did not wait until 1918 but resigned that summer.[66]

Barker's resignation was a huge loss for the university athletic program. For more than two decades he had sheltered and nurtured the program. He had shielded it from Patterson's wrath and had tried to instill some sort of fiscal stability. He had been the football team's biggest fan, cheering from his private box at home contests and traveling to away games. When notable victories prompted a jubilant nightshirt parade, he frequently went along "entering fully into the spirit of the celebration."[67]

Barker was also an unceasing supporter of the student body, tolerating, if not always condoning, student high jinks. He was remarkably quick to defend the students against all criticism—even when they had indeed gone too far. After the 1913 victory over Cincinnati, for example, many UK students "let their enthusiasm get the better of their discretion." They poured through downtown Lexington, pulling trolleys off line, highjacking several beer wagons, and carrying off theater lobby signs. Police attempts to break up the near-riot proved fruitless. Once again, Barker went downtown and persuaded the students to return to the campus. As always, Baker defended their actions as mere high-spiritedness. He stated, as so often before, that a university without spirit was dead.[68]

During the Barker years, athletics established a firm foothold within the university structure. Football especially rose to greater popularity, and thousands of fans regularly filled the bleachers at Stoll Field. A few trends from this brief era are clearly seen. During this time, the university football team outgrew intrastate competition. Of forty-seven games played, only nine involved in-state opponents. The Wildcats won eight of those games. Despite at times being "hopelessly outclassed" against national powerhouses such as Vanderbilt or Illinois, the team managed to win 70 percent of its games. UK fans often took comfort in hard-fought losses at the hands of strong teams, while at times criticizing the team in victory.

More than anything, the fans lived for the occasional upset. Notable in this category were victories over Purdue, Tennessee, and Mississippi State. The 1914 Mississippi State game became known in local lore as "the greased pants game." The first half of the contest ended with the visitors from Starkville ahead 13-0. Throughout the half, UK players and coaches complained to the referees that the Mississippi players had greased their pants in an effort to elude tacklers. The officials made the visitors change uniforms at halftime. Thereafter, they failed to score while the Wildcats piled up nineteen second-half points to win.[69]

Despite the progress made in athletics during the Barker years, some primitive elements still survived. Throughout the period, key varsity players made a habit of skipping all or part of the two-week practice session before the season began. Also during this time, scheduling difficulties continued to be common. In 1911, for example, a last-minute cancellation forced UK to play its October 21 game with the Lexington High School.[70] In 1916, the Wildcats were idled for two consecutive weeks because of cancellations. The University of Louisville canceled its November 9 game with UK because too many of its players had either been injured or declared ineligible.[71] The Cats received an extra week's rest when Marshall also canceled its game. Disagreements between UK and Marshall were common at this time. Their 1913 clash did not materialize because of an irreconcilable argument over the eligibility of several Marshall players.[72]

Barker's last year saw the arrival of S.A. "Daddy" Boles as assistant coach. Boles served in a number of capacities, including head football coach, athletic director, and business agent. During his long stint, he provided much-needed continuity for a program that suffered from constant turnover in the coaching ranks. During Barker's six years, for example, the Wildcat football team had four head coaches.[73] Barker's most enduring legacy was his adoption of the new athletic board. He designed this ten-member advisory board to insulate athletics from unfavorable administration opinions. It would prove to be an institutional framework that his successor would not easily dismantle.

THE EARLY MCVEY YEARS

What do you say if we forget the past and derive a little pleasure in pipe dreams of the future?

—UK student yearbook[1]

BEFORE SCHOOL RESUMED in the fall, the board of trustees suc-ceeded in appointing a successor to Barker. Instead of promoting one of its own as it had done in 1911, the board selected Frank L. McVey, formerly of the University of North Dakota. The new president quickly found that he had inherited several difficulties relating to the athletic department. For starters, a controversy had arisen that spring con-cerning J.J. Tigert. In view of his athletic duties, Tigert had requested an additional year of leave from his position as chairperson of the phi-losophy department.

The dean of arts and sciences, however, did not look favorably upon the request. As he told the board, such leaves "had a tendency to cause the work of teaching to disintegrate." Dean Miller wanted Tigert to return to his academic post. He and the trustees discussed the mat-ter at some length. Miller indicated that when Dr. Tigert had divided his attention between football and philosophy, "his teaching work had not been entirely satisfactory." On the other hand, acting chair Glanville Terrell had filled the position quite admirably. If Tigert returned to the classroom, would he resume his previous post or would Terrell continue as chair? Some board members were of the opinion that Tigert should remain in the athletic department, some thought that Terrell should keep the department head position, while others believed that if Tigert returned, he was entitled to the top post. In typical fashion,

Richard Stoll moved that the board appoint a committee to study the matter. Without further discussion, the board adopted this motion.[2]

Before long, the newly arrived McVey quickly became involved in this matter. He sided with Miller; thus Tigert found himself back behind the lectern full-time. S.A. "Daddy" Boles assumed the twin tasks of head football coach and athletic director. Jim Park, former quarterback and now ex-professional baseball player, became his assistant, making for a rather sparse staff.[3] The football season that ensued produced the first losing record in nearly two decades. As the yearbook noted, "the grim visage of war" had cut a wide swath through the South. Nine starters from the 1916 team heard the call to arms, and the ranks were further thinned by an outbreak of measles.[4] At the University of Tennessee, so many of the Volunteers had in fact volunteered that it could not field a team. The Wildcats had to arrange another foe for Thanksgiving. To no avail, Boles tried to stir up enthusiasm for the replacement game with the University of Florida. A smaller crowd than usually attended a UK-UT game watched the Wildcats rout Florida 52-0 for one of only three wins during the season.[5]

The next year brought no improvement in athletic fortunes. In fact, it could well be argued that 1918 produced the strangest season in UK history. The war in Europe raged on unabated and indirectly produced a torrent of change at the university. In late September, military officials announced that it would move the National Army Training Detachment stationed at nearby Camp Buell to the UK campus and consolidate it with the Student Army Training Corps (SATC). These twelve hundred men were divided into two groups. Company A consisted of university students, while the much larger Company B contained soldiers receiving crash courses in vocational skills such as auto mechanics, carpentry, blacksmithing, or electrical engineering. Barracks constructed on the east side of campus were to house the men.[6]

At first, die-hard football fans welcomed this influx of new personnel. The War Department announced that it would allow—in fact, encourage—the soldiers to participate in intercollegiate athletics, provided that road trips or practice did not interfere with drill or study. The student newspaper thought that this decision (a reversal of an

President Frank L. McVey

earlier order) brightened the outlook for UK athletics tremendously. Captain H.N. Royden, commanding officer of the SATC, issued a personal statement encouraging all SATC members who were skilled in the sport to try out for the Wildcat football team. He reasoned that the training given on the football field was also excellent military training.[7] Such optimism proved to be short-lived. The UK team did record a notable 27-0 shutout of Indiana at Bloomington, but the influenza epidemic sweeping the country brought wholesale changes to the Lexington campus. In early October, the *Herald* reported that the flu was spreading through military encampments around the nation with incredible speed and fury.[8]

Influenza often spread quickly, but the epidemic of that year differed from previous outbreaks in several key respects. First, its spread was greatly facilitated by the worldwide movement of troops fighting in World War I. Second, no other type of influenza before or since had such a capacity for developing complications from pneumonia, the real

SATC Company B reports for training on campus, 1918.

culprit behind most flu-related deaths. In fact, a great many doctors at first thought that this disease was something much more devastating than mere influenza. Some physicians guessed that the ancient pneumonic plague had made its way to America from North China, where it had recently decimated much of the population.[9]

The epidemic had actually begun in the spring, but by the early fall, it had escalated into a virtual pandemic. The disease killed as many soldiers as died in World War I combat and ten times that number of civilians. Most frightening of all, this strain of the disease struck hardest among those in the prime of life. Flu epidemics generally killed only the very young or the very old. The 1918 pandemic, however, behaved entirely different. Records from all over the country reveal that the hardest hit group consisted of those twenty to twenty-nine years old. All available knowledge of the disease's normal course shouted that this could not be, but the truth was inescapable.[10]

The inability of physicians to cure or even to treat the outbreak only added to the great sense of foreboding. In most cases, antibiotics or, for that manner, any medical practice of the day proved ineffectual in fighting either the flu or pneumonia. The general method of treatment called for doctors, or most often nurses, to provide warm blankets, food, and fluids and hope that the patient stayed alive until the disease ran its course.[11] The military was the first agency carefully to record the impact of the disease. In some areas, most notably Camp Devens in Massachusetts, the death rate in army camps was as high as ninety per day.[12] Table 1 reveals the spectacular and frightful toll the disease exacted among young soldiers. Quite suddenly, those areas of the country that had military camps had great cause for alarm.

At the University of Kentucky, those observers who had greedily eyed the SATC soldiers as fodder for the football team now viewed the maze of temporary barracks in a different light. So too, did certain city and state officials. Although the *Kernel* noted on October 4 that there was no influenza on campus, optimism was in short supply. On October 8, the State Board of Health issued sweeping closing orders for Lexington. Specifically, the board ordered all public schools, universities, and places of amusement closed. The ordered closing of horse racing's trotting season generated a great deal of opposition. Many of those involved fled south for the more congenial political climate of Atlanta, where the Georgia State Board of Health announced that it would not interfere with the sport. The military used the now-vacant Lexington facilities to house more soldiers.[13]

The health agency also forbad people from traveling to the universities. Accordingly, only those Transylvania or UK students already in campus dormitories or barracks could continue their classes. Those students living outside the grounds and those who had gone home could not return to Lexington to resume their studies.[14] The next day, the Herald reported the first flu-related fatalities in Lexington. It also noted that the first case had been diagnosed in Patterson Hall, one of UK's two women's dormitories. President McVey was greatly alarmed and canceled the football home opener scheduled for October 11. He also wired Washington, D.C., asking for a ruling from the War Depart-

TABLE 1
Flue and Pneumonia Deaths among Soldiers
Stationed at American Posts

Week beginning:	# Deaths
September 6	40
September 13	36
September 20	98
September 27	972
October 4	2444
October 11	6170
October 18	5559
October 25	2624
November 1	1183
November 8	908
November 15	519
November 22	21
November 29	319

Source: Alfred W. Crosby, *America's Forgotten Pandemic: The Influenza of 1918.* (New York: Cambridge Univ. Press, 1989), 59. According to Crosby, the Army demoblized in November so quickly that its mortality statistics after that date are less accurate.

ment on the seven hundred SATC men who had been living in town awaiting the completion of the Rose Street barracks. McVey did not want them on campus, but the War Department was unsympathetic to his appeal.[15]

Within a few days, the disease had established a stronghold in town. The Board of Health counted nearly three hundred cases of flu in Lexington and more than one hundred at UK. McVey responded with what he hoped would be decisive action. The students from the collegiate branch of SATC (Company A) were rushed through their induction and then hastily furloughed, transferred to other camps, or sent to officer training schools. As the two campus infirmaries quickly filled, McVey ordered that the gymnasium be converted into a hospital under the guidance of Mrs. W.H. Thompson, superintendent of nurses from nearby Good Samaritan Hospital. Soon, the gymnasium became a convalescent ward where recovering patients were moved to make room in the infirmary for the more extreme cases. The university also moved the women students out of the newer dormitory and placed it "entirely at the disposal of the State Board of Health." The women, crowded into one dormitory, received their academic instruction in the cafeteria.[16]

McVey again locked horns with the military. At first, he tried to convince the officials in the nation's capital to transfer the remaining SATC soldiers to other bases. The telegram sent from the War Department indicated otherwise. Officials there stated that all SATC men must remain in college until completing their courses. Dr. John South, president of the State Board of Health, also tried his hand at blocking the next shipment of SATC soldiers to the UK barracks. He reasoned that if students were not allowed to return to the campus, then surely it was unwise to have seven hundred new men brought into Lexington. This plea also fell on deaf ears, and the soldiers reported according to orders, fueling another small outbreak of the flu.[17]

After twice vetoing it, the health agency finally lifted part of the flu ban, allowing the university to reopen. No sense of normalcy accompanied this action. By that time, the only students on campus were those in the new SATC Company B and the long-suffering students essentially held hostage in the women's dormitory. The football team managed to play two somewhat ill-advised away games, but McVey forbad any home contests. This included the annual Thanksgiving Day game, prompting the *Herald* to proclaim that for the first time in years, the Wildcats and their fans could "eat their turkey in peace and true Puritan tranquility."[18]

Campus flu victims fill the gymnasium.

Thanks in part to the quick action of McVey and others, the influenza epidemic touched the university only lightly. Out of 403 cases of flu and 14 of pneumonia, the college suffered 8 fatalities in the SATC barracks. One of the flu fatalities had been complicated by measles. McVey put these figures in perspective by noting that the University of Michigan had suffered 50 deaths. Nationwide, the death rate in the regular war cantonments averaged 10 percent, compared to 2 percent at UK.[19]

The university fared even better than the city of Lexington, which itself was not really hard hit. There, the Board of Health reported 1,248 cases of flu and 52 deaths, with an additional 35 related deaths attributed to pneumonia. These figures did not take into account the

Eastern State Asylum on the edge of town, which suffered 28 deaths. According to the *Herald,* the southern and southeastern regions of the state were greatly affected. In Breathitt County, for example, more than 2,000 cases of flu had been recorded, and the city of Jackson was in panic.[20]

What the *Herald* did not reveal was the heavy toll the pandemic exacted in Louisville. According to statistics compiled by historian Alfred Crosby, the Falls City was the second-hardest-hit city in the entire nation. Unlike Lexington, which was more isolated, Louisville was a major river port and center of commerce and transportation. The flu, like the pioneers of another century, moved across the country by following established trails. In 1918 these trails were railroads and rivers, and Louisville was a major center for both. Also unlike Lexington, Louisville suffered three major and separate outbreaks: in October, December, and March.[21]

The city did not adopt the extreme measures imposed upon the citizens of Lexington or even other major commercial port cities. For decades, prominent health reformer and noted Lexingtonian Linda Neville criticized the Louisville health officials for being too lax.[22] As a result, the river city did not escape the pandemic as did some areas of the Bluegrass. During the month of October alone, the city suffered more that 450 flu-related fatalities. For the last four months of 1918, the Kentucky death rate per thousand was 4.4. Yet, in Louisville, the figure stood at 8.1. Its death rate trailed only Pittsburgh's 9.2.[23]

The waning of the flu epidemic coincided with the end of World War I. The armistice forced the trustees to decide how to proceed with the rest of the academic year. Some trustees favored dividing the forthcoming spring into two quarters to make up for the lost fall semester. The majority, however, voted to return to the regular semester schedule. The board then granted a full semester of credit to all SATC Company A students and women students, as well as any students who returned to farms to produce food for the war effort or who left UK to work in defense plants. For the spring semester, Company A cadets continued their military drill until June 30. Their military duties were lightened and their classroom hours lengthened.[24]

In January, the students bid a fond farewell to the maze of SATC barracks. At the same time, the administration eagerly looked forward to a check from the War Department, which indicated it would reimburse the university for the cost of lodging, feeding, and instructing the soldiers. The university maintenance staff promptly tore down the last vestiges of the wartime occupation. The students were gladdened that the armistice had come and the flu had left in time to salvage the spring sports season. Reflecting on the virtually nonexistent football season, the yearbook editor earnestly hoped that the former letter winners would be discharged and able to return in time for fall practice.[25]

After the flu interruption, athletic fortunes at the university did not improve. The 1920 yearbook summed up matters succinctly, declaring that sports were "not a phenomenal success." For the 1919-1921 period, the football team posted records of 3-4-1, 3-4-1, and 4-3-1. Indicative of this level of success, the game hailed as the greatest battle of the era was a loss to Vanderbilt. What made it such a notable contest was that it was the first time that UK had ever scored against the team from Nashville. In typical fashion, the yearbook editor denounced the team's performance the next week—a 33-0 victory over Georgetown College. The record improved in 1922 to 6-3, thanks in part to a softer schedule and an upset win over Alabama.[26]

In this gloomy environment, the 1923 season ushered in a truly dark chapter in the early history of UK sports. In that year, the school suffered its first athletic fatality. In the second game of the season, junior center Price Innes McLean received a sharp blow just over his left eye—an area not covered by the primitive helmets worn at that time. After the hit, he lined up for the next play without apparent trouble but was unable to remember the play signals. With the help of the right guard he was able to snap the ball back to the quarterback. He played out the quarter, and at halftime the coaches wrapped cold towels around his head. Some observers stated that he occasionally lined up slowly and paused as if to catch his breath. Still, no one thought his injury to be serious. After the game, he dressed and left without assistance.

The next day, he ate breakfast with the team but, complaining of headaches, he decided to return to bed. At noon his teammates noticed that he was still sleeping and tried to awaken him without success. They rushed him to Good Samaritan Hospital one block from the campus where doctors performed emergency surgery, which they at first declared successful. At 7:30 that evening, however, the twenty-year-old McLean died from a cerebral blood clot.[27]

At first there was a great deal of uncertainty about the team's future. The *Herald* had reported similar fatalities from around the nation for several decades. In each case, the affected team had disbanded for the year, whether voluntarily or by administration decree. The paper noted that the athletic council would meet that morning (Monday) to decide on a course of action.[28] On the day of the funeral the council reported that it had decided to continue with the football season. It noted that "curtailment would be of no possible benefit to the young man or his family and it would be difficult to change the schedule already laid out."[29]

At the campus memorial service, thirteen Wildcat football players carried McLean's casket into the university chapel. President McVey presided and opened by reading from Psalm 91. Speaking for the athletic department, professor Enoch Grehan stated that McLean had "died in service for the university and in no better way can our recollection of his worthiness be proved than to carry on his burden where he left it and to do as well as he did."[30] The team limited its official mourning to the suspension of one practice. Team members echoed Grehan's sentiments that the best tribute they could pay to their fallen teammate would be "to play out the schedule as if nothing had ever happened and make the season the success that McLean had hoped for." The team indeed played out its schedule of games, rallying to tie Washington and Lee four days after burying McLean's body.[31]

Some of the more callous souls on campus feared that McLean's death would have a negative effect on plans for a new football stadium. The same issue of the *Kernel* that so solemnly recounted the memorial service also reported (on page one) that plans for the new stadium were being rushed through. The student author anticipated that the U-shaped concrete stadium holding twenty-five thousand fans would open on time for the 1924 season opener.[32]

A larger and more modern stadium had been the fervent hope of Wildcat football fans for the better part of two decades. After several false starts, the stadium plan had finally begun to materialize the previous spring. The biggest obstacle faced by supporters of a new facility was the resolve of President McVey that the university could not afford to fund such a project. It was abundantly clear, therefore, that the money would have to come from outside the university. This lack of financial support from the administration did not deter the Wildcat faithful. The student newspaper noted that numerous southern colleges had conducted successful fund-raising drives to build stadiums. Specifically the *Kernel* noted that University of Georgia students had contributed $172,000 and University of Alabama students had raised $150,000 in their campaigns.[33]

In April, the students and faculty began a campus-wide fund-raising drive, hoping to collect $25,000. Within a few days, they succeeded beyond their expectations. Students and faculty raised a total of $34,253. The engineering department, soon to play a vital role in designing the stadium, contributed the most to the project. One hundred percent of its members donated, averaging $26.46 per student. The greatest number of contributions came from the women's division, whose students gave an average of $18.27.[34] The campus contributions, although inspiring, were not nearly enough to fund the entire project. The university's growing alumni association provided the bulk of the funds. By May, it had organized the Greater Kentucky Fund with the goal of raising $200,000 to build a new football stadium and, if possible, a new basketball arena.[35] The university and the alumni association entrusted the stadium plans to the school's civil engineering department headed by Professor Daniel Terrell. As originally designed, the stadium resembled a smaller version of the Ohio State University facility. The plans called for a U-shaped stadium consisting of sixteen sections capable of seating 25,000 fans.[36]

By late fall, the parties involved were optimistic enough to select a site for the new stadium. Among those discussed were Scovill Park, the old jail property, and several spots on the UK experimental station farm. The planners rejected these potential locations because they were too far from campus. In the words of the *Kernel,* a stadium built on one of these sites "would not really appear part of the university." Attention then turned to Stoll Field. Some critics noted that building on the east end of the area would destroy the picturesque botanical gardens. Debate continued until spring, with the alumni and athletic council settling on the western edge of Stoll Field as the most suitable building site. Those plans received a severe blow in April when the trustees, athletic council, and stadium committee met to discuss the matter. The trustees and McVey believed that the west end location entailed expensive sewage problems. Mayor Hogan Yancey (former Transylvania football star) attended the meeting and stated that he would be glad to cooperate in the construction of the sewer. Yet he could give no assurance that the city could afford such a project at that time.[37]

At this point, the board's executive committee left the meeting and inspected the proposed sites. After a lengthy discussion of sewage, which Professor W.D. Funkhouser, representing the Athletic Council, claimed would be a problem either on the west or east end, McVey redirected the discussion. He noted that the western site required extensive grading, which might be too costly. He proposed that the stadium be built on the eastern edge of Stoll Field (along Rose Street) because it was fairly level. With two dissenting votes, the various committees approved this proposal. They recommended that the builders not disturb the existing playing field and wooden bleachers, in case the new stadium could not be ready in time for the fall season.[38] A few weeks later, the university awarded the stadium contract to the Louis des Cognets Company, a Lexington-based concrete and construction company.[39]

The expectations of some fans crashed headlong into reality. Those followers who had hoped for the biggest stadium in the south were very disappointed with the changes made in the stadium's design. By the time construction began, the stadium committee had scaled down its original plans. The funds raised for this project could not cover the expense of the sixteen-section horseshoe design. Instead, des Cognets set about to build a much smaller five-section stadium—two sections along the north side of the gridiron and three along the south side, with a seating capacity of 8,500. University officials promised that the remainder of the structure would be erected as funds became available.[40] On a brighter note, the construction went very smoothly and under budget. In fact, the university had enough funds left to take advantage of a contractual clause wherein des Cognets had offered to build a sixth section at a reduced rate. The construction company further helped out by donating a thousand dollars to the project. The board of trustees thanked Professor Terrell and the stadium committee for an admirable job, noting that the new stadium "reflected great credit" upon the alumni and the university.[41]

As the *Kernel* described, "a new stadium made possible through the efforts of the alumni of the university greeted all old students when they returned." This assessment was not totally accurate. By the time of the October 4 Louisville game, the stadium was barely half finished. The fans for this first home game all sat in the nearly finished stands on the south side of the field. Two weeks later the fans filled the completed southern section, and a few hundred sat in the northern stands, which were still under construction.[42]

Wildcat fans eagerly anticipated the completion and dedication of the stadium, scheduled for the November 1 clash with Centre College, UK's most popular rival of the 1920s. As planned by the stadium committee, Captain C.C. Calhoun of the alumni association would formally present the stadium to the university. Richard Stoll would accept it on behalf of the board of trustees. The band would play the national anthem and "My Old Kentucky Home." Then, the committee would unveil two bronze tablets: one honoring Stoll and one honoring Kentucky soldiers lost in the World War.[43]

Before November 1, a major change took place in the proposed ceremonies. The UK student council requested that the stadium be named after Price McLean. Some Wildcat followers thought that the stadium should be named after Richard Stoll and that fitting tribute could be paid to McLean with another bronze tablet.

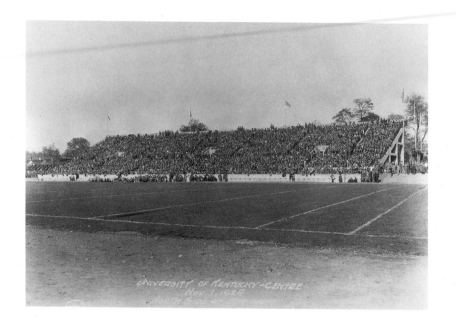

First game played in McLean Stadium, UK v. Centre, 1924

The dedication ceremony produced the season's largest crowd. The fans had only taken up about half of the available room for previous games (see table 2). An overflow crowd, accommodated in wooden bleachers, observed the dedication ceremonies and then watched as UK lost to Centre, 7-0.[44]

Although the university did adopt the title McLean Stadium, it did not gain universal acceptance. For years, many fans held on to the older and familiar name of Stoll Field. Many of them made reference to McLean Stadium at Stoll Field. Official university maps often listed both names. One revisionist *Kernel* editor, writing in 1936, claimed that both the field and the stadium had been named in honor of Judge Stoll, but "a bronze plate commemorating Price McLean's death was placed at one end of the stadium and since that time it has been known as McLean Stadium."[45]

These first eight years of McVey's long presidency were the least

TABLE 2
Attendance at Home Football Games, 1924

Date	Opponent	Capacity	Tickets sold
Oct. 4	Louisville	5,200	3,004
Oct. 11	Georgetown	5,200	3,051
Oct. 18	Washington and Lee	8,600	5,160
Nov. 1	Centre	10,400	12,033
Nov. 15	Virginia Military Institute	10,400	2,385

Source: "M'Lean Stadium is Really Stoll Stadium," *Kernel*, 24 January 1936, 36.

successful in the school's early sports history. The football program suffered its first losing seasons in two decades, winning only twenty-nine of sixty-three games (46 percent). Yet, the program survived in spite of the calamities that befell it. Moreover, the new president, not nearly the fan his predecessor had been, at least tolerated sports. His complaints were few, and as yet he showed little inclination to involve himself or to assert a greater authority in the matter. That would await a later day. On the other hand, certain developments within the limited women's athletic program captured his keen attention.

BANNING WOMEN'S SPORTS
AT THE UNIVERSITY
OF KENTUCKY

These bitterly fought contests are certainly not conducive to the health of our girls.

—Sarah Blanding, UK dean of women[1]

WITHOUT DOUBT, basketball is the signature sport at the University of Kentucky today. The first organized team on campus, however, was not the now famous men's team (discussed in the next chapter) but rather the women's team. An examination of the history of women's sports on the campus reveals many insights into American social values in general. It showcases the long-standing bitterness that existed between physical education departments and competitive sports, and it clearly demonstrates how a national movement played out in a local setting.

Available information indicates that women students often developed sporting activities long before physical education departments found a place for them in the official curriculum.[2] In response, women physical educators acted quickly to exert professional control over any student-run athletic clubs. At the University of Kentucky, the relationship between the sport of basketball and the physical education department was never happy. Florence Stout, women's physical education director, tried at first to maintain the sport as a very limited element of her overall program of instruction. Stout feared, as did many other people in her position across the country, that if the game made the transition from a gym class exercise to a varsity or intercollegiate

94

sport, the position of physical education within the school would decline. Most often at coeducational institutions, the transformation of the game into a competitive sport brought along with it professional coaches outside the control of the physical education departments. Stout's fears materialized during the 1909-1910 academic year. At that time, the administration removed women's basketball from her strict supervision and transferred it to the athletic department.

For nearly fifteen years Stout fought against this decision. An examination of this topic not only highlights American social thought in action but also reveals a great deal about the political structure of the university. It suggests the lengths to which a struggling department would go when it perceived an interdepartmental threat. No clearer example of an academic political fight, or "turf war," existed in the university's early years. It also provides a vibrant example of a tactical and political argument in operation. Key women in the university administration waged a long and ultimately successful attack on women's sports on the grounds that women were too frail, both physically and mentally, for the rigors of the game. Did they really believe their own doctrine of womanly weakness, or did they adopt this argument knowing that it would appeal to a wider audience? Did this tactic conceal the true political motives at the heart of the attack?

Regardless of motives, the irony here is pervasive. Nineteenth-century women's activists had campaigned against the medical doctrines that announced that women could not endure education without risking permanent harm.[3] Yet, women physical educators of the 1910s and 1920s used similar arguments to warn that competitive sports would cripple women athletes. How could an era so characterized by the campaign for equal rights coexist with a campaign to limit opportunities for women athletes? Why did women's physical educators proclaim that women lacked the physical and mental stamina for competitive sports?

In its earliest years, women's basketball existed as a minor adjunct of physical education. It came to the University of Kentucky campus somewhat later (1902) than at the northeastern schools, just as formal physical education did. During the nineteenth century, President Patterson was content to let military drill serve as the only form of required exercise for the male students. For twenty years, no similar program existed for women students. Not until late 1901 did the board of trustees finally vote to form a physical education department open to both men and women students. Patterson, intent on saving money, had planned to hire a men's instructor who would have the additional responsibility of teaching women during the men's military drill hour. Over his objections, the board hired two instructors, one for men and one for women. They accomplished this task by taking advantage of Patterson's absence from the December 1901 meeting owing to illness.[4] The members chose Florence Offutt Stout to fill this new post. Stout belonged to a very prominent Bluegrass family of the time and had recently returned to the state having earned a diploma from the prestigious New Haven Normal School of Gymnastics.[5]

Someone, presumably a board member, leaked this news to Patterson, who arose from his sickbed to reprimand the trustees. With rather sharp rhetoric, he informed the board members that the $30,000 grant from the general assembly would not cover the actual building expenses of the new gymnasium. The already tight budget could not bear the further strain of two physical education instructors. In equally sharp tones, he further reminded the board that the executive committee had, six months earlier, settled the issue by hiring the male instructor to teach all students. The board stood by their actions of the previous day but did compromise with Patterson on a fiscal point. They agreed to an annual five-dollar-per-student gymnasium usage fee, which they had previously opposed.[6]

Stout proved a sound choice. Among her converts was Patterson himself. Having once argued that gymnastics were unladylike, he now praised the women's physical education department in general and Stout in particular. He praised her knowledge, enthusiasm, and the "sound principles of her instruction." He conceded that the success of the women's department had, in fact, "fully justified" the board's decision. Renewing her contract, the board also approved final plans for construction of the university's first gymnasium.[7]

The gymnasium opened on time in the fall of 1903, but unfortu-

*Women's physical
education director
Florence Offutt Stout*

nately, the women's stay in that facility was brief. In December of that year, monitress (the position predating that of dean of women) Lucy Blackburn wrote to the board protesting circumstances relating to the gymnasium. She told the board that coeducation, difficult under the best of conditions, had become even riskier with the opening of the gymnasium. She noted with alarm that whereas women were barred from the building unless supervised by Stout, the prohibition was regularly evaded. Men and women students had been ignoring classes and even chapel services to meet clandestinely "in the building to chat and waltz together."[8]

While as yet no true scandal had occurred, the situation made her quite anxious. She did note that the committee on college discipline had already reprimanded several students and dismissed one young woman from school "for violation of the regulations relating to their presence in the gymnasium during forbidden hours." Blackburn urged the board "to throw all safeguards possible around the young women." Among these was the transfer of women's physical education from the gymnasium to the women's dormitory. She conceded that this made certain facets of athletic training—most notably basketball—impossible. "But," she explained, "we want to promote Physical Culture in the girls and not to make athletes of them."[9] The board, moved by Blackburn's argument, and fearing a possible scandal, promptly ordered the transfer.[10] Stout bitterly complained about this relocation, but to no avail. Thus, the women's department of physical education began a twenty-year sojourn in temporary and generally substandard facilities.[11]

At that time women's basketball was a very minor element of the physical education program. It continued to be so until the campus armory was floored, providing another place to play. Stout disliked the game, preferring a more conservative approach to physical education, which she labeled "medical gymnastics." Very common in the mid- and late nineteenth century, this form of exercise required students to perform light calisthenics upon the command of an instructor.[12] Yet, noting her students' interest in the sport, she included it in the official curriculum under her careful supervision. For most of the first decade it was limited to an annual interclass scrimmage. The team did play a few intercollegiate games with nearby colleges, but only on Stout's strict terms. She believed that spectators created too much tension, and she refused to allow male students to watch the games, believing it to be improper.

Stout's position on this matter led to one of the most unusual episodes in university history. In 1904, Herman Scholtz, a UK student, disguised himself in women's clothing and accompanied the women's team (presumably with their knowledge and cooperation) to witness their game with Georgetown College. Stout discovered his presence about halfway through the game and became incensed. She attempted to bring disciplinary charges against him, but the faculty senate was at a loss as to how to proceed. It seems that masquerading in women's clothing was not among the seemingly countless rules of student conduct. Even so, Patterson reprimanded the imposter on "general principles."[13]

Apart from that occasion, women's basketball attracted very little

The University's first basketball team, the 1902-1903 women's team

attention until it became the focal point of a university-wide power struggle. In November 1909, the faculty senate heard a petition on behalf of the team, signed by team manager Alice Carey, team captain Bessie Hayden, and seventy-three other coeds. The petition complained that Florence Stout stifled the development of the sport, and they requested that "the control and management of the Girls' Basketball Team" be turned over to the athletic association. The faculty approved this arrangement.[14]

To shore up support, Hayden appeared before the executive committee of the board of trustees the next day. She read a similar statement, requesting that the team be made part of the athletic association. Upon a motion made by Richard Stoll, the committee unanimously approved the request.[15] Florence Stout, however, did not approve. She wrote a strong letter of protest to Patterson, who in turn read it to the executive committee. The committee, in typical fashion, decided to stall and appointed a subcommittee to look into the matter and take any action it deemed appropriate without having to report back to the full committee. Yet it is rather clear that the matter was not really up for debate, as indicated by the choice of Stoll as subcommittee chair.[16]

At first, the athletic association did not know how to react. Association head A.M. Miller reported to the faculty senate that the women's basketball team had asked permission to travel to the University of Cincinnati to play a game. Miller told the senate that he was unsure if his association had the power to grant the request. Patterson replied that it did not, and would not, until the executive committee ruled on the issue.[17] Two weeks later, the senate reported that the executive committee had indeed upheld the transfer of the team to the association. The subcommittee attempted to appease Stout by giving her the power to judge the students' fitness for the sport. If she deemed a coed unfit for basketball, that student would have to withdraw from the team without appeal.[18]

This attempt at compromise did not placate Stout. She appeared before the senate and "entered into a somewhat extended discussion of the relation between her, the athletic association, and basketball games." She complained that wresting the team away from her had nullified her influence among the young women of the university. In a long tirade, she argued that the game of basketball was entirely too severe for young women and must, therefore, be strictly supervised by a trained professional. The minutes stated tersely that she cited "numerous authorities" to support her views.[19] Unmoved by this argument, a faculty representative then read a lengthy statement from the athletic association stating that the management of women's basketball had not been sought by the association but rather imposed upon it by the administration. To that end it would work to schedule games with other teams while always acting in the best interests of "the welfare of the young women."[20]

This argument raged for another month. At the next senate meeting, Patterson attempted to reverse the previous decisions. He read a resolution giving Stout the exclusive right (by virtue of her twin positions as head of physical education and dean of women) to rule on any matter related to women students. Her decisions would be "paramount and without an appeal except to the board of trustees." He also stated that the faculty should publicly express regret for this "unfortunate difference of opinion which has arisen between the athletic association and the head of the department of physical education in regard to their respective spheres of jurisdiction." His resolution met with resounding defeat.[21]

Noting this development, the student yearbook stated that in the spring of 1910, the university's women athletes "after some skirmishing . . . withdrew from the protective care of Mrs. Stout and allied themselves with the athletic association, thus becoming an important factor in our athletics."[22] In protest, Stout resigned her position as dean of women, calling it an ornamental title with no real authority. In a letter to the board, she stated that she would seek a greater usefulness in physical education and did not want irrelevant administrative duties to distract her from her true life's work.[23]

Any additional hopes that the administration might soon reverse its decision crumbled when Patterson retired and the board appointed Henry Barker to succeed him. If anything, the next years saw a steady erosion of Stout's authority. Her long friendship with the former president now became a liability. In 1911, at Barker's suggestion, the board lowered her salary from a recommended $1,200 to $1,000. The next year, the finance committee proposed an annual salary of $1,700, but the board cut it to $1,100. One year later, Barker stated in his president's address that "the directors of physical education for both men and women are relatively overpaid in comparison with similar departments in other universities." He offered no proof for this statement, but the board apparently needed none. Again, they voted to cancel another proposed raise for Stout.[24] In a clearer personal attack, Barker ordered Stout to repay the money she had earned from the use of the university swimming pool. Under a program instituted by Patterson, Stout had been allowed to charge for private swimming lessons to nonstudents.[25]

When the women's basketball team was taken away from the women's physical education department, it was then supervised by the athletic department. The 1914 team was coached by J.J. Tigert.

Largely because of Barker's support of athletics and his rather vindictive personality, Stout's attempts to curtail women's athletics failed. Indeed, the Barker years saw the expansion of women's athletics. After the athletic department was established, it provided a coach for women's basketball (usually an assistant football coach), thereby completely removing Stout's department from the picture.[26] The governing of women's basketball remained the same until certain personnel changes occurred in the university. Two changes especially shaped the school's policy concerning women's athletics. First, Barker resigned quite suddenly in the summer of 1917. As it turned out, new president Frank L. McVey was not the staunch supporter of women's athletics that Barker had been.

Emboldened by the change at the university's helm, Florence Stout decided to test the political waters. She began subtly, without actually mentioning women's basketball or her unsuccessful earlier campaigns against it. In February 1918, she wrote to McVey with the results of her latest screening of freshmen women. She informed the president that of all the problems that engaged her attention, the increase in "nervous diseases among the young women of the University . . . [was] the most disquieting to say the least." She suggested that the remedy for this alarming condition could be found in a "re-education of the will" through gymnastics, religion, prayer, and, if necessary, electric vibration treatments. Additionally, she reported that nearly 60 percent of the new women students lacked the necessary lung capacity for strenuous exercise.[27]

Her next and in many ways most crucial action came in 1920. She wrote to McVey suggesting that women's athletics be removed from the athletic department and placed under control of a women's athletic council consisting of the dean of women, director of women's physical education, assistant professor of women's physical education, and two additional members (one faculty, one nonfaculty) appointed by the president. As proposed, and eventually adopted, the council would "make plans for the further development of the athletic side of the women's life at the university." It would also "schedule all intercollegiate games and determine the conditions which shall control such games."[28] This step was of immense importance because it allowed Stout and her associates to attack women's athletics without having to confront the athletic department.

A week later, McVey wrote to dean of women Josephine Simrall stating that he supported the "plans for the development of the athletic work among women." He also wrote that he would like to discuss the matter with other people "before going into the matter thoroly [sic.]."[29] With that letter, the matter appeared to be dropped. Finally, in the fall of 1923, he wrote to Stout stating that he too opposed women's intercollegiate sports. He believed it would be better to encourage intramural sports among a broader group of students rather than fostering competition for only a few varsity team members. He suggested that she discuss the issue with her staff to see what would be "best under the circumstances."[30]

McVey's letter delighted Stout. She replied that for years she had fought "single-handed and alone in the university against intercollegiate games, and all basketball activities for girls not directed and safeguarded at every step by the physical education director for women." She informed the president that her earlier campaigns had met with defeat because the athletic department, "composed of men, stood solidly against me, even though I was backed in my views by national authorities." She concluded by stating how refreshing it was to learn of McVey's sympathetic views.[31]

A second personnel change in 1923 greatly enhanced the campaign against women's athletics. At that time, Sarah Blanding received an appointment as Stout's assistant. Blanding had come to the university four years earlier with a diploma from the New Haven Normal School of Gymnastics. She enrolled seeking an undergraduate degree in political science. After graduation, she worked as women's physical education instructor and then in 1923 became dean of women, a position she held for nearly twenty years before leaving the university to accept the presidency of Vassar College.[32]

Stout and Blanding made a formidable team. With a monopoly on the woman's athletic council, and with McVey's blessing, they were finally able to abolish intercollegiate sport in the fall of 1924. In September, the woman's athletic council recommended to the university senate that women's sports be discontinued. The senate, however, did not rule on the motion at that time.[33] In an interview for the *Kernel,* McVey explained the reasoning behind the proposed ban. He stated that he and others believed that intercollegiate basketball had "proved to be a strenuous sport for boys and was, therefore, too strenuous for girls." In addition, he continued, the team's road trips had become too expensive "because of the necessity of proper chaperonage." He claimed that already there had been some unfortunate consequences as a result of such travel and he believed that it was no longer desirable "to have girls in the university travelling over the state and throughout the South in order to take part in intercollegiate sport."[34]

The timing of the ban proved to be nearly perfect for Stout and Blanding. Supporters of the women's team within the athletic department were happily building both a new basketball arena and a new football stadium and raised no protest. These construction projects provided quite a diversion. Indeed, the *Herald* article describing the proposed ban on women's athletics was only two paragraphs long. The unrelated second paragraph detailed the seating arrangement for the new stadium.[35] The construction also provided a reason for some supporters of women's varsity to reassess their position. The athletic department greatly needed money. Thus, it is not terribly surprising that athletic director S.A. Boles would tell McVey that he believed intramural sports for women would be more beneficial than intercollegiate competition.[36] The women's basketball team, once a prized trophy, was now a fiscal liability.

The proposed ban did not, however, go unnoticed among the students. A *Kernel* editorial lamented that abolishing women's sports would mean a great loss to the school, a loss of the patronage of town and campus supporters, and a destruction of a great deal of school spirit.[37] The paper claimed that the student body, especially the women, were strongly in favor of retaining women's varsity basketball. It noted that a petition signed by 200 women students (of the 735 enrolled) would be presented to the senate at its next meeting, when the issue would be decided.[38]

For a brief moment, hope flickered. The *Kernel* reported that the senate had granted a hearing regarding the proposed ban. At the next meeting, the women players would be allowed to speak, and "the plea of the girls" would be considered.[39] That opportunity never came. Instead of the students, McVey, Blanding, and Stout appeared before the senate and in unison recommended that the administration ban women's intercollegiate sport. Addressing the meeting, Blanding stated that one leading national physical education organization, the Women's Division of the National Amateur Athletic Federation (NAAF), was on record as being opposed to intercollegiate athletics for women. In addition, she noted, the Conference of American College Women and the National Association of Directors of Physical Education for Women had "also taken a definite stand against intercollegiate competition for women." Blanding further claimed that 93 percent of collegiate administrators nationwide opposed varsity sport for women. The senate approved the recommendation, and as the *Kernel* recorded, it abolished intercollegiate sports for University of Kentucky women on Thursday, November 13, 1924.[40]

All traces of varsity competition promptly disappeared from women's sporting activities. Stout's department quickly took control of basketball, tennis, field hockey, and track, ensuring that the students' competitive spirit would be carefully and properly regulated. Unlike many other colleges and universities, Kentucky did not at first adopt the play day format endorsed by the NAAF and the American Physical Education Association (APEA). Under this arrangement, women from various schools met at a host campus. Then they were mixed into nonpartisan teams for carefully supervised games.[41] By Stout's decree, women's intramural basketball also disappeared. She believed that this form of competition fostered bad manners. The intramural format did not return to the university for nearly ten years.[42]

In 1928, Blanding wrote to McVey assessing the women's program under the new guidelines. She was pleased to report that the women's athletic association had fulfilled physical education's national goal of "a game for every girl, and every girl playing a game." Now that Kentucky, "like most of the colleges in the country . . . [had] given up the varsity team with its emphasis on star players," they had been able to accomplish the "bigger purpose of having every girl participate in some sport." Blanding further claimed that the ban on intercollegiate basketball had, in fact, produced better athletes. She proudly noted that women could still earn what used to be called a varsity letter. Previously, letter awards went only to a small number of gifted athletes who excelled in one sport, namely basketball. Now, the award was based upon a system whereby students earned points by demonstrating proficiency in a variety of sporting activities, supervised, of course, by the physical education department. A student needed one thousand points to receive the award, and any woman who earned her "K" had clearly proved that she was an all-around athlete.[43]

With the passing of intercollegiate basketball, the role of the women's athletic association changed greatly. With no varsity or intramural matches to arrange, the association turned its attention to nonsporting social events. For nearly ten years, its chief enterprise consisted of organizing campus dances.[44] This pattern continued for a remarkably long time, in large part because of the stability and continuity of leadership involved. Blanding served as dean of women for nearly twenty years. Stout chaired her department for more than forty years.

In this instance, as is often the case, it is easier to describe the chain of events than to explain the motives behind it. The membership of Stout and Blanding in organizations such as the NAAF and the APEA offer a glimpse at motives. Yet national policy alone is not sufficient to explain the Kentucky case. For example, historian Ellen Gerber pointed out that on a national or institutional level, the NAAF's animosity toward sport grew out of a dispute with the American Athletic Union (AAU) concerning the control of women's track and field. In 1922, the AAU sent a team to the Paris Women's International Athletic Games. Gerber noted that women's physical educators disapproved of these plans but were unable to influence change. In response, they "withdrew from AAU committees, refused to serve in the future, and created their own organization to control women's athletics."[45]

In Lexington, however, opposition to women's sports did not

begin suddenly in the 1920s. Florence Stout lobbied vigorously against competitive athletics for more than a decade before the NAAF launched its campaign. Additionally, there were no references to the AAU, either in her correspondence or that of Blanding. At the University of Kentucky, national goals received reinforcement from a number of local concerns and sentiments. It is rather easy to spot some of Stout's motives for opposing sports. Her letters to the president and board of trustees seethe with professional and departmental jealousy. She greatly resented the favored status of sports on campus. For years, her classes were shuttled around to temporary facilities. Conditions became so bad in spring 1924 that the wooden structure used for women's gymnastics was declared beyond repair. The superintendent of buildings and grounds told the board that the building could not be used at all—not even for storage purposes. It was torn down and the materials sent to the shop to be used as scrap.[46]

Women's physical education finally found a permanent home in the fall. At that time, the new basketball arena opened, and the men's department of physical education left the old gym for quarters in the new building. Indicative of the second-class status accorded to women's physical education nationwide, the women's program moved into the vacated building from which they had been banned two decades earlier.[47] Stout frequently complained that women's physical education needed more outdoor facilities, such as a hockey field, tennis court, and track. The university never found the money for her programs. On the other hand, it did find the thousands of dollars to fund the twin sports projects of the 1920s—new men's basketball and football arenas.[48]

Less is known of Blanding's objections to women's athletics, mostly because her stint as dean of women began less than a year before the women's sports ban. Blanding was an active member of both the NAAF and the APEA, which were the most outspoken opponents of women's sports, especially denouncing all intercollegiate and Olympic competition.[49] Judging from her official papers, Blanding kept in contact with prominent members of the NAAF and could be counted on to support the national platform, which condemned competitive sports as undemocratic, exploitive, and dangerous.[50] The most compelling argument issued by the NAAF against sports centered on the issue of women's health. In its national platform and in numerous publications, it claimed that women had neither the physical nor the mental stamina needed for competition.

These charges centered on the notion that women could not bear the strain of competition. Age-old concerns that excessive activity (especially running and jumping) would damage reproductive organs surfaced frequently. Indeed, the *American Physical Education Review* (*APER*), published by the APEA, reprinted a *Journal of the American Medical Association* article warning that an athlete's uterus was "liable to displacement by the inexcusable strenuosity and roughness of this particular game [basketball]." Accordingly, the *APER* pronounced that any achievement made by women on the basketball court was not worth the potential health risk.[51]

Opponents of competitive athletics often tried to prove that women were not natural athletes but were driven into sports by untrained male coaches. When women were not under the close supervision of trained women's physical educators, they could be pushed beyond their limits, physically and especially emotionally, to satisfy coaches, sponsors, and crowds. For example, Helen Coops, director of physical education at the University of Cincinnati, wrote of a ghastly women's basketball tournament where men jeered at the women players who were attired in "abbreviated costumes." The pace of the game was so great that several women had to be removed from the floor in fainted or hysterical conditions. The crowd continued to urge the remaining competitors on with shouts of "Fight! Fight!"[52]

According to many women's physical education instructors, competition was so dangerous that women had to be protected from it at all costs. Thus, educators frequently tried to dismiss the popularity of sports among their own students. Logic here implied that young women could easily be exploited and pushed to injury by an uncaring, untrained male coach. For their own good, therefore, women had to be protected against these coaches and against their own misguided desire to compete. To that end, the NAAF adopted a platform that called for having "well-trained properly qualified women in immediate charge of all athletic and physical education activities."[53]

Blanding's correspondence indicates that she did indeed support this national platform. For example, in December 1923, F.B. Lambert, superintendent of a West Virginia school district, wrote to Blanding asking her opinion of athletics for high school girls. She responded by imploring him not to adopt interscholastic sports. Blanding warned that "the strain and excitement attending these bitterly fought contests are certainly not conducive to the health of the girls." She noted that physical injury posed a constant threat, but the nervous strain produced by competition was particularly devastating and not easily overcome. She urged Lambert further to make sure that all aspects of girls' exercise be closely controlled by "a good physical director from some reputable school of physical education."[54]

Blanding's position on women's athletics is, however, more than a little ironic. During her undergraduate years, Blanding played on the University of Kentucky women's varsity basketball team. Ten months before writing to Lambert, Blanding was the subject of a Lexington newspaper article. In previewing the forthcoming basketball game with Louisville, the *Herald* noted that women's coach A.B. "Happy" Chandler (future baseball commissioner, U.S. senator, and Kentucky governor) was confident that his team could avenge the earlier defeat against Louisville. The newspaper pinned its hopes on UK captain Sarah Blanding, whom the paper called the best player ever in the state. The UK team did in fact defeat its Louisville opponent by the score of 18-6. Blanding scored fourteen points.[55]

A strong case can be made that there was another meaning just beneath the surface of physical education rhetoric. It is difficult to explain how women's physical education instructors could adopt repressive beliefs of women's limits unless they viewed this strategy as the most powerful way to attack the sports programs outside their control. Perhaps they embraced these theories, aware that a large audience would be receptive to them. Despite the talk of "the new woman" and the revolution in social thought in the 1920s, older beliefs of women's frailty clearly lingered. Seeking a powerful argument in their

The 1923 women's basketball team, captained by Sarah Blanding (center, with ball), and coached by then-law student Albert "Happy" Chandler

battles against competitive sports, professional coaches, and athletic departments, women's physical educators were happy to tap into this anxiety for their own political gain. Otherwise it is inconceivable that Sarah Blanding could have believed that basketball would destroy the health of University of Kentucky women. After all, most of her life to that point was a living contradiction of her own argument. Her swift and remarkable conversion to this tactic only underscores the political realities of the athletic ban.

Many physical educators did in fact adopt and repeat these pronouncements from the NAAF. Helen Coops certainly did. Anna Norris of the University of Minnesota also warned that basketball could destroy the health of women athletes—especially if directed by male coaches who had no respect for feminine physiology. She claimed to know many women who had sustained permanent "pelvic difficulty" as a result of basketball tournaments. Such instances led her to declare that athletics could not be carried on safely "as long as women were women." In a letter to Blanding, Norris wrote that unless changes were made in women's sports, the athletes would be "butchered to make a Roman holiday."[56]

There may indeed have been a great deal of solidarity within the ranks of women's physical education. Yet such opinions were not universally shared by those outside organized physical education. The athletes themselves disagreed; so did their coaches. Moreover, the United States Olympic Committee disregarded the NAAF's many petitions to ban women's participation in the Olympic games.

Some have argued that the physical educators against competitive sports advanced theories about the ruination of young womanhood not because they believed them but rather because they were graphic and alarming. The NAAF's national platform contained over one dozen objections to competitive sports. Yet the one used most often in the national media, and the only argument advanced at the University of Kentucky, focused on the crippling effect of sports on young women. Such reasoning was far more compelling and effective than merely attacking varsity sports as undemocratic or of dubious educational value. Furthermore, by focusing on an impending crisis in women's health, physical educators could claim that they were acting heroically to safeguard young women—not simply their own professional hegemony.

The abolition of women's intercollegiate sports in the 1920s was ironic. In this case, organizations and departments headed by women acted to limit sporting activities for other women. Numerous motives, at both the national and local level, can be studied in search of an explanation. Yet, whatever the motive, the result at the University of Kentucky was that women's competitive sports did not return to the campus for fifty years.

From Humble Origins to Signature Sport

In the days B.R. (before Rupp) basketball and chinese checkers held about the same athletic rating at Kentucky.
—1939 UK student yearbook[1]

FEW SPORTS IN THE NATION today enjoy the lofty reputation and rabid following of University of Kentucky basketball. Yet like many of the major sports at the university, basketball can certainly point to very humble origins. As was the case with UK football, it took the better part of two decades for basketball to establish itself as a viable sport and major element of the school. For most of those years, it owed a great deal of its existence to football, which provided most of the players and all of the coaches for the indoor game.

Other than a later start (invented in 1891), basketball's origins closely resemble those of college football. The same Charles Eliot who had many times called for the end of football when he was president of Harvard also urged his university to abolish basketball. Eliot claimed that the roundball sport had became even more brutal than football. There was more than a kernel of truth to his charge. As historian Bert Nelli has described, early basketball games were slow-moving defensive battles where the score often remained in the twenties. College teams were usually composed of football players who frequently possessed only a rudimentary knowledge of the game. Fouls were rarely called, and the spectators often went home disappointed if robbed of the chance to see a good on-court fight.[2]

The sport's development on the UK campus also mirrored patterns seen years earlier in football. Specifically, the same student-run, student-financed origins are clearly evident. Before the administration and faculty became involved, the team manager controlled all aspects of the sport. He scheduled games and practices, distributed tickets, collected all revenues, and paid the bills. Resources were also meager for basketball as they were for football. Just as the football team was frequently unable to buy all the necessary equipment, the basketball players had to contribute twenty-five cents each toward the purchase of a ball. This three-dollar investment must have been difficult to arrange, as the team possessed only one ball, which they used for both practices and games.[3]

The biggest difference seen in the evolution of the two sports involved playing facilities. In the early years, money was the critical ingredient for maintaining the program. Without administrative financial support, the funds had to come from ticket sales. In this respect, football enjoyed a great advantage over basketball in that it was played outside, where paying fans could sit in temporary bleachers. Finding a place to play was more of a challenge for the indoor sport.

For its first twenty years, the team played in the gymnasium, which opened in 1903. The facility, located in what is now Barker Hall, had to be shared by both men's and women's basketball, as well as physical education. In addition, the football team and users of the swimming pool had to share the basement locker room facilities. The gymnasium itself consisted of a playing floor and a running track suspended overhead. The builders clearly did not intend the gym to host closely followed intercollegiate games. Most notably, it had no real seating capacity. The only fans that could watch a basketball game were those fortunate souls who found standing room on the running track. At most, the track could safely hold a few hundred spectators. For important contests, the overflow crowd spilled outside the building. Generally someone with a megaphone provided updates for those fans not fortunate enough to get inside the building.[4]

From such truly humble origins, the sport climbed to national prominence. Yet, the earliest years of basketball were far from glorious, or even mildly successful. The first seven years played under the student manager system produced a record of twenty wins and thirty-

The men's basketball team played its games in the women's gymnasium.
Spectators stood on the suspended running track.

three losses, a winning percentage of just over 37 percent. As was the case with football, the whole basketball program on occasion seemed on the brink of collapse.

That moment almost came in the fall of 1909. In November, the faculty finally addressed a common complaint. For several years, various groups on campus had complained about overcrowding in the gymnasium.[5] The many organizations that needed access to the building had been unable to draw up a schedule agreeable to all concerned. On November 19, the faculty athletic committee shocked the student body by voting to abolish men's basketball to alleviate the overcrowding. The committee based it decision on the team's lack of practice time and poor record. It stated that things were "better never done than half-way done."[6]

The student newspaper reported that this decision had indeed stunned the student body. It admitted that the gym had been overbooked but had anticipated the committee granting the team more practice time by doing away with something else—most likely physical education. As to the criticisms of the basketball team's record, the *Idea* blamed the losing record on the lack of a coach. According to the student sportswriter, the football team had demonstrated the value of a good coach. Unfortunately, the student body could not afford to hire a basketball coach, and the school officials were not willing to do so. The paper urged the students to "go after the faculty, the trustees, and if necessary the legislature for a new gym."[7]

The students also presented the faculty with a more feasible suggestion. Shortly after the committee announced its ban, the students presented a petition to the board of trustees requesting that the maintenance staff install a wooden floor and better lighting in the armory. This action would alleviate some of the gymnasium overcrowding. The trustees approved this suggestion and took quick action. By the end of the Christmas vacation, the maintenance department had finished the renovations, and the winter basketball season began on time.[8]

Much to the delight of basketball fans, the team received another of its most cherished wishes—a coach. Football coach E.R. Sweetland announced that he would take over the basketball coaching position. The hopes for a successful season, however, were quickly dashed. In the wake of a 4-8 season, many fans searched for an explanation. The student yearbook took an extremely critical stance, blasting the players for the losing season. It noted that

> after the armory was floored, there was ample time for practice, but the old men, the men who ought to have been the strength of the team did not take up the game with the proper spirit. When they did train, it was in a half-way manner. They thought that as long as they showed up once or twice a week for practice they had their place on the team cinched. The new men were made to think this and they never tried as hard as they might. Then when the time came to make the trip North, a number of the men were behind in their work and could not

go. Consequently the trip was taken only with a scrub
team, and we lost all the games. After the inglorious slump
of this season, let us all take a brace and bring out basketball to the standard of our other athletics.[9]

UK fans suffered through another dismal season in the absence of
Sweetland. His triumphant return in the spring of 1912 brought about
the team's first undefeated season. The Wildcats tore through the nine-
game schedule, never losing and, in fact, never trailing. It handily defeated all KIAA opponents as well as Ohio University, Vanderbilt, and
Tennessee. The students gave credit to Sweetland for this turnaround.
The yearbook stated that the whole season bore "the impress of the
magical hand of Coach Sweetland." He filled the players with confi-
dence, trained and instructed them as only he could, "and as is his
invariable custom, turned out a championship team."[10]

That level of attainment was not to be repeated anytime soon. As
mentioned previously, the 1912 season was Sweetland's last at the university. In terse prose, the *Kentuckian* noted that the basketball season had been marred by "a very dark cloud of difficulties and obsta-
cles." Because of the events surrounding the Webb trial, including the
time spent by Sweetland in court, preseason basketball training
was canceled. After Sweetland's late January resignation, his successor,
J.J. Tigert, inherited a young, inexperienced, and out-of-shape team
that nonetheless managed to post a modest winning season.[11]

Barker's formation of the athletic department did a great deal for
the minor sports, which included basketball at this time. By providing
a coach, the department granted the sport a modicum of stability during these years and carried it through the tougher times, especially
after the resignation of Sweetland. During the next several years, football coaches Tigert, Park, Brummage, and Boles each took a turn at
coaching basketball. They provided competent, if not always outstanding, leadership and posted a very credible collective 50-32-1 record
(60 percent) over the course of seven seasons.

The hiring of George Bucheit (sometimes spelled Buchheit or
Buckheit) illustrated a trend that lasted for more than a decade.[12] First,

Bucheit was hired as an assistant football coach with the added responsibility of coaching basketball. During this period, all of Kentucky's basketball coaches did double duty (at least) for the athletic department, coaching football as well as other minor sports. It could well be argued that their football backgrounds were far more important than their basketball resumes. Bucheit, however, had been a two-sport star in college.

Second, Bucheit played his undergraduate sports at the University of Illinois. Kentucky's basketball coaches in the 1920s (with the exception of UK alumnus Basil Hayden, hired at the last minute for the 1926-1927 season) came from Illinois. At that time the Illini football program was among the best in the nation. Under famed coach Robert Zuppke (who coached there from 1913 to 1940), the team dominated the Big Ten conference and earned a sterling national reputation. It should be noted that Bucheit was not the first in the long line of Illini men to coach at UK. S.A. "Daddy" Boles came in 1916, and over the course of several decades served in various roles. The 1917 yearbook described him as "a product of the far-famed Zuppke system."[13]

Regardless of whether he was the first coach to bring the Big Ten style of play to Lexington, Bucheit is generally considered the first major coach to help elevate UK basketball to a higher level. He employed a strategy known as the "three man attack" in which he stationed one player under each basket. The remaining three players covered the rest of the court.[14] His strong point was his ability to inspire his players and mold them into a close-knit unit. In his five years at UK, Buchheit posted two losing seasons: 5-7 in 1920 and 2-10 in 1923. The 1923 team produced the second-worst record of that era. In actuality, Bucheit's winning percentage of 60 was no better than the combined totals of the Tigert/Brummage/Park/Boles coalition. His reputation, however, is forever secure because of events that transpired in early 1921.

The 1920-1921 Wildcat team, although young and not highly regarded, lost only once during the season. More important, it was the first UK team to make a reputation for itself outside the confines of the state. That spring, the young team, led by the shy and soft-spoken Bucheit, not only received a rare invitation (fifteen teams in the South were so honored) to the SIAA tournament, but won it as well. In the final game against the University of Georgia, Kentucky tied the game with seconds remaining, thanks to the heroics of team captain Basil Hayden, described by the *Kentuckian* as "a blond Apollo, a Kentucky thoroughbred, if one ever stepped on the turf." First-year player Bill King then won the game from the foul line with no time left on the clock.[15]

Hundreds of UK fans had packed into Lexington's Phoenix Hotel for telegraphed reports of the game. A hotel employee provided periodic updates to the crowd by using a megaphone. Upon hearing news of King's foul shot, the assembled throng erupted in wild applause.[16] The celebration continued through the night and, in some places, the entire next day. On the UK campus, students cut classes in what the *Herald* called "the most unanimous prodigality ever known." The few students who did attend classes could not hear above the celebration taking place outside. Professors, therefore, had no choice but to declare a holiday. Fearing that the festivities might turn destructive, university authorities called out the military, who locked up the armory and the gymnasium.[17]

Although the team returned all starters, it was unable to recapture the magic of 1921. Hayden injured his knee during the track season and returned the next fall as only a shadow of the basketball player he had been. Compounding matters, Sam Ridgeway, also a star in 1921, missed the entire season because of illness. The 1922 team finished with a 9-5 mark, including an early tournament loss.[18] Bucheit stayed on for two more years, posting records of 3-10 and 13-3. Although asked by the athletic department to stay, he chose to leave UK and continue his coaching career at Duke University (then known as Trinity College). The athletic department filled this vacancy by hiring C.O. Applegran, another Zuppke product.[19]

By the early 1920s, the basketball program was just beginning its evolution into one of the nation's best. It was abundantly clear to a number of observers that the team had outgrown its playing facility.

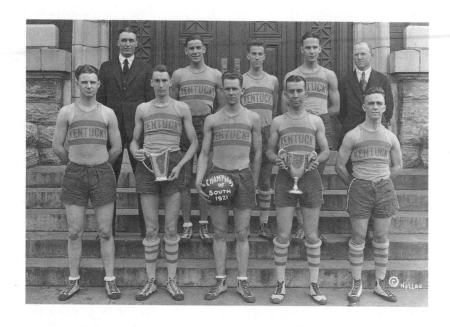

Basketball coach George Bucheit (back row, left), assisted by S.A. Boles (back row, right) pose with 1921 Southern Tournament champion basketball team. Star player Basil Hayden is pictured holding game ball.

Some people on campus even feared that the gymnasium might prove to be unsafe and unable to hold the crowds that packed the suspended running track. UK fans, especially those among the alumni, renewed their hopes for a more modern gymnasium. In January 1923, athletic council representatives, headed by Professor W.D. Funkhouser, appeared before the board of trustees to discuss the matter.

Funkhouser stated that the athletic council, the alumni, "and others interested in athletics at the university" believed that it was the proper time to begin construction of a new athletic arena. Dr. Funkhouser discussed various plans to raise the necessary funds for the project. He told the assembled trustees that the council would greatly appreciate "some sort of statement from the executive committee as to its attitude." After some discussion, the trustees adopted a resolution indicating that they were "in sympathy with the purpose of the athletic council."[20]

Even with the board's sympathy, a number of factors complicated plans for a new gymnasium. Foremost among them was President McVey's stated reluctance to build any athletic facilities. He did not see such construction as a high-priority issue. If the administration was going to approve the spending of tens of thousands of dollars, he believed the money should go toward faculty raises. He told the board that the school was losing some of its younger faculty because UK salaries were lower than those paid at benchmark institutions in other states. He could not advocate spending large sums on the sports program while there existed "a distressing need for increases in the salaries of regular professors."[21]

Earlier proposals for a new football stadium further complicated the issue of the new gymnasium. McVey questioned the feasibility of raising enough funds for one project, much less both. Supporters of the new arena were thus convinced that they would have to raise money from outside the campus. One trustee suggested that the board, which planned to ask the state legislature for $110,000 for the construction of a World War I memorial, should pad their request. If that sum could be increased, perhaps to $200,000, then the administration could divert the excess to the gymnasium. McVey thought this was a terrible idea. He stated that requesting money "solely for our varsity teams would not be popular in the state and even among the alumni, as I see it."[22]

McVey's opposition did not deter the athletic department. Two months later it again appeared before the board and delivered a more formal request. Again, Funkhouser served as spokesperson and presented the following petition.

1. The interest and attendance in basketball has reached the point where the university can no longer accommodate the players or spectators.
2. This results in a financial loss each year amounting

William D. Funkhouser,
head of zoology department,
dean of the graduate school,
and athletic council chair

to several thousand dollars and discourages the support which the university should receive.

3. The present gym is unsafe for the crowds which attend the games and can not be used as an adjunct to field sports.

4. The university has built a fine organization in interscholastic basketball; this year 154 teams of various parts of the state competed for the high school championship. The final tournament is held at the university and brings large numbers of high school boys and girls to the campus. Conditions, however, are so discouraging to these teams that an effort is now being made to take the tournament away from the university and hold it in Louisville. We feel that this would be most unfortunate but believe that this brings the basketball situation to a crisis.

5. The present undefeated basketball team (the interscholastic champions of the United States last year) will be the varsity team next year and has a very strong local following. Since the interest in our team will, therefore, be unusually great, it seems that now is the logical time to provide a suitable building for games and tournaments.

6. The athletic council, therefore, begs the board of trustees to consider the proposition of borrowing enough money to build a building costing from $15,000 to $20,000 for this purpose, the money *to be repaid* by the athletic council in installments from the proceeds from basketball games. We believe that the increased profits in the sport would pay for the building in ten years.

7. The type of building suggested is a stucco-covered frame and steel building of the style of which a plan is herewith submitted.

After some discussion, the board members indicated their support for the new building but stated that the administration "was powerless to borrow money for purposes of this kind."[23]

Throughout the spring and summer, the alumni association rallied around the issue of the new gymnasium. By July, it felt confident enough to request the board to approve a site for the building, pending an agreement on how to finance the project. The athletic council, alumni association, and trustees decided that if the proposed building should be located along the western edge of Stoll Field bordering on Winslow Street (what is now the corner of Euclid and Limestone).[24]

By October, the alumni association had convinced the administration that it could raise the money necessary for construction. On October 2, 1923, McVey granted permission for the alumni association to sign a contract with the builder for the foundation of the new facility. The $20,000 required for this phase would come from the alumni association's recent football stadium drive. The association estimated the total cost of the project at between $54,000 and $60,000.

It assured McVey that it could easily produce an additional $20,000 from the same drive. The athletic council pledged to finance the remainder with basketball gate receipts, which Funkhouser expected would total $10,000 per season.[25]

At this point, the alumni scored a major victory when McVey approved another of their requests. In order to prevent any delays in the start of construction, the association urged McVey to advance $20,000 in anticipation of the alumni fund drive. To further pacify the still doubtful McVey, the alumni-athletic department coalition included in their plans a monument for the late James K. Patterson and a student loan fund. The president agreed to this arrangement, noting that the revised plans for the gymnasium would produce "a more satisfactory building" than he had anticipated.[26]

This happy accord was not, however, unanimous. The university business agent believed that it was not a good time to begin such a project. He informed McVey and the board that the school's budget was stretched so tight that the school might not be able to meet its financial obligations. "In the event," he warned, "that any large amount has to be paid on account of the Basket Ball Building, I am not at all sure we shall have sufficient funds to meet our current expenses." If the administration persisted with this project, then "it would be well for the board today to make some provision for such an emergency." This warning went unheeded, and the trustees approved the formal contract with the alumni association, athletic council, and the Blanchard-Crocker construction company.[27]

Unlike with the McLean Stadium project, which came in under budget, things quickly went wrong in the construction of the new arena. First, between July and December the cost estimate ballooned from $56,000 to $90,000. Next, the contractor encountered severe financial problems, and for a while it appeared unable to finish the project. To that end, the university "found it necessary to assist the contractor by endorsing notes to the amount of $20,000," leaving the contractor to carry the balance. This bad news once again prompted many alumni and trustees to covet the money reserved for the war memorial. In April 1924, the board loaned the athletic council $50,000 from the memorial fund.[28] Even this amount did not prove to be enough. By the end of May, the contractor had essentially gone bankrupt, stopping all work on the building. This action left the university with more than $15,000 in liens. It also left them with an unfinished building, which required the school to spend more money. Almost immediately, the administration found itself besieged with law suits from unpaid subcontractors.[29] These actions left the athletic council/alumni coalition with a debt far in excess of the original estimate. The new building, eventually renamed Alumni Gymnasium, may have been the pride of the four thousand fans who packed it to watch the Wildcats, but it crippled the finances of the coalition for decades to come. It also did a great deal to poison the relationship between athletics and McVey (as discussed in greater detail in the next chapter).

Unfortunately, the new campus monument to basketball fever did not guarantee instant and uniform success. The first year in the new arena produced a 13-8 record and an early exit from the tournament. The yearbook editor complained that the team lacked consistency and played "a rather mediocre brand of ball." The student annual hoped that with all starters returning next year, the team would become "accustomed to the big floor at the gym and Coach Applegran's system."[30]

That chance never materialized. Applegran chose not to return for the next season, and to fill this vacancy, the athletic department hired another Illinois graduate, Ray Eklund. Eklund had been a multisport star for the Illini. In addition to his basketball duties, he also served as assistant football coach.[31] Under Eklund, the team's record improved somewhat to 15-3. The students described this version of the Wildcats as "the greatest team that has worn the Blue and White since the Southern Champions" of the 1920-1921 season. After losing the first two games to DePauw (of Indiana) and Indiana University, the team sailed through the remaining schedule before losing to Tennessee in the tournament semifinal.[32]

As was the case entirely too often in the 1920s, UK soon found itself looking for a new coach. Shortly before the 1926-1927 season opened, Eklund resigned quite unexpectedly, citing ill health.[33] Some

Alumni Gymnasium

followers of the sport believed that he despaired seeing only one returning starter and a shocking lack of depth. Sensing an inevitable
losing season, he fled. At such a late date, the athletic director could
not find an established coach to take over the program. It was not until
December 1, with the season opener looming near, that the *Herald*
finally announced that the athletic council had at last hired a coach. At
this late date, the university prevailed upon 1921 hero Basil Hayden to
come aboard the sinking ship. The newspaper hinted that Hayden had
not been the council's first choice for the job. It also speculated that
his stay in Lexington might be short, as indicated by his contract, which
expired at the end of the season.[34]

Hayden did have some coaching experience (at Clark County
High School and Kentucky Wesleyan College), but had decided earlier that he did not particularly like the profession. His experience
during the next few months only reinforced that belief. For starters,
his salary, rumored to be "liberal," was meager by any standard. The

Basketball coach John Mauer

board of trustees voted to pay him only three hundred dollars per month for a three-month period, less than $1/7$ the figure earned by the football coach.[35] The team received very little preseason training, lacked experience, and had no depth, being composed primarily of first-year players. It proceeded to lose more games than any UK team of this era. Against thirteen loses, the team showed only three wins. Perhaps, the *Herald* theorized, asking a new coach with a new system to work with green materials was just too much to expect. Particularly loathsome to the UK faithful were the losses to nearby rivals Georgetown College and Kentucky Wesleyan, not to mention the 48-10 loss to Cincinnati. The Wildcat's 3-13 record did not merit an invitation to the postseason tournament. Once more, Hayden decided that coaching was not for him, and he left Lexington.[36]

With more time to review candidates for the position, the athletic department chose another Illinois graduate to revive the basketball program. Thus, John Mauer became the fifth UK basketball coach in as many years. As were many of his predecessors, Mauer had been a multisport athlete at Illinois, where he had played in the same backfield as Red Grange, the most famous football star of the day. Also like his predecessors, he served as an assistant football coach. Mauer faced the daunting task of rebuilding Kentucky's basketball fortunes. His one returning veteran, Paul Jenkins, missed most of the preseason practices because of his participation on the football team. Mauer was very disappointed in the level of play exhibited by his charges during the preseason. But he patiently taught and the young team quickly learned enough to post an 11-6 record, earning a tournament invitation where the dark horse Wildcats surprised many spectators by advancing to the semifinals before losing to the University of Mississippi.[37]

Mauer's style of play was characterized by an impenetrable man-to-man defense and what some observers termed a "slow-breaking offense" featuring short, quick passes. He also employed "a submarine attack," which involved the use of the new bounce pass.[38] Over the next several years, Mauer's teams compiled an enviable record, winning 74 percent of their games. The only dark blot on his UK career was his failure to win the tournament championship. The closest the team came to this pinnacle was in 1929 when it suffered a heartbreaking loss in the finals. The University of Georgia won by two points as a last-second UK shot spun out of the rim.[39]

Mauer's stay at UK was short. After the 1929-1930 season, he decided to continue his coaching career at Miami University of Ohio. His stay at UK was bittersweet. He posted a very good record but failed to win the coveted championship. He was well-liked by his players but disdained by the press, which claimed that he lacked the ability to stir his players up into a frenzy for big games. In the long run, his most unforgivable sin occurred in 1939 when he moved to Knoxville to perform double duty for Kentucky's most hated rival—the University of Tennessee. Mauer, perhaps more interested in football than basketball, became a scout for Tennessee's famous gridiron coach, Robert Neyland. He also took over the Volunteer basketball program, becoming Kentucky's major nemesis.[40]

In May, "Daddy" Boles extended a contract offer to a coach at Freeport High School in Illinois. This coach, Adolph Rupp, accepted the offer and on May 31 the board of trustees approved his appointment "as instructor in physical education, to have charge of varsity basketball and to assist in other sports." His first-year salary totaled $2,800—$500 less than Mauer's 1929-1930 salary and about half of the head football coach's yearly pay.[41]

Unlike many of his predecessors, Rupp had graduated not from Illinois but rather from the University of Kansas, where he had played for noted coach Phog Allen. Rupp had been a member of Allen's 1922 national championship team. After graduation, Rupp first coached at Marshalltown High School in Iowa, where he had charge of football, track, wrestling, and basketball. In addition to his Freeport High School ties, he also had an important, if indirect, Illinois connection. It is doubtful that UK would have hired him without the strong recommendation he received from Illini basketball coach Craig Ruby.[42]

Rupp's years in Lexington have become legendary. He coached the Wildcats from 1930 to 1972, winning an astonishing 82 percent of his games. In addition, his teams won eighteen SEC titles and four National Collegiate Athletic Association crowns. Many fans eagerly anticipated a new style of play under Rupp. The *Kernel* announced in May 1930 that UK could now "bid farewell to its well-known submarine and delayed offense employed by Coach Mauer." Rupp advocated "the fast break system which is the most popular style used in basketball at the present."[43]

Whether Rupp actually brought a totally new brand of basketball is a matter of some debate. It was, however, quickly apparent that he brought an entirely different personality to the program. Rupp instituted grueling practices and enforced strict discipline. He was not the patient teacher that Mauer had been and had little use for players who had not already mastered the game's fundamentals. Also unlike Mauer, Rupp really did not seem to care if his players liked him and made no pretense of friendship with them. It may well be that he had no close friends within the program. Yet the fans embraced this dour man with his many idiosyncrasies and superstitions. The press especially took to Rupp, who seemed always ready with a quotable quip.[44]

During Rupp's first season at Kentucky, he was greatly aided by the low expectations of the Wildcat faithful. Few fans believed that the new coach could produce good results with a team hard-hit by

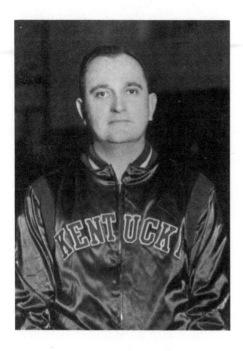

*Basketball coaching legend
Adolph Rupp*

graduation. They were very pleasantly surprised, therefore, when the 1930-1931 edition of the Wildcats finished the year 15-3. Even more surprising, the team advanced to the tournament finals, losing a two-point decision to the University of Maryland.[45] Over the course of the next years, Rupp sustained this level of success. During his first ten years, the coach won 82 percent of his games, won the postseason tournament four times, and saw numerous Wildcat players receive All-Conference and All-American honors.

As a result of Rupp's outstanding record, a curious revisionism settled over Lexington. Specifically, fans seemed to forget entirely the fine contributions of Mauer. In a 1939 student yearbook article, Joe Creason claimed that before Rupp arrived, "not enough customers attended the games to furnish sides for a fast game of two-eyed cat. The teams were groping along with mediocre success playing the slow-breaking game that is so characteristic of Southern basketball."[46] Such a dire pronouncement hardly did credit to Mauer's 74 percent winning record. Nor did it provide adequate testimonial to the keen alumni interest that spearheaded the drive for the new arena.

Some writers have downplayed Rupp's initial success by indicating that his teams played an easier schedule than the football team. They note that the SEC, especially after it split from schools such as North Carolina, Duke, and Maryland (which in turn formed the Atlantic Coast Conference), was more renowned for its football.[47] There is a good deal of truth in this allegation. Kentucky was in the conference forefront in the amount of attention given to basketball. In addition, there was clearly a lack of quality coaches in the South at this time. Many SEC teams were coached by a succession of assistant football coaches who may not have really enjoyed, or even understood, the nuances of the game. Additionally, most schools granted very few basketball scholarships. Consequently, many basketball teams continued to be composed of football players.

Yet, it must still be remembered that the Wildcat's nonconference schedule included some of the nation's top teams. The university basketball team frequently did battle against such schools as New York University, St. Joseph, Michigan, Notre Dame, and Marquette. Two of those games particularly stand out in the team's early years. During the 1934-1935 season, the Wildcats traveled north to play NYU. The Kentucky team may have possessed the finest arena in the South, but it did not compare to the fabled Madison Square Garden. There, before 16,538 fans, Kentucky lost a narrow decision, thanks in part to some questionable officiating, which drew criticism from many corners.[48]

The 1938 contest with Marquette had a different ending and also lived on in local lore. With time running out in the contest, Wildcat Red Hagan sank a basket from beyond midcourt. The Alumni Gymnasium crowd exploded into wild cheering. To mark the occasion, Governor A.B. "Happy" Chandler, in attendance that evening, drove a nail into the floor at the spot where Hagan had unleashed his shot.[49]

Basketball rose to great prominence at Kentucky under the tutelage of Coach Rupp. Yet, as the 1930s drew to a close, it was evident that this trend was just beginning. Throughout most of the South, and in many ways at UK, basketball was still subservient to football. Among

Early in his UK career, Adolph Rupp (second from left) also served as an assistant football coach. Head coach Harry Gamage is pictured wearing dark jacket. Bernie Shively (second from right) later became athletic director.

the SEC teams, the Wildcat program was clearly the first to assert some independence from the gridiron sport. This proved to be a slow process, and throughout the decade, Rupp continued to wear many hats at the university. It would be years before the athletic department freed him from his other teaching and coaching duties to concentrate solely on basketball. Rupp's salary increased during the 1930s, but it still only amounted to about half of that paid to his football counterpart.[50]

Basketball's rise in the 1930s coincided with quite the opposite development in football. Soon, the program that had survived many scrapes would again run afoul of the administration. Unlike the basketball team, however, which had risen from minor sport to consuming passion, football would suffer a most crushing blow—loss of alumni support. Discontent in these quarters would finally give McVey the leverage he needed to institute what he believed to be long-needed reforms. Basketball and Coach Rupp would be virtually the only elements of the program to escape his wrath.

EXPANSION, DEPRESSION, AND FISCAL CHAOS

And he thought within himself saying, what shall I do, because I have no room where to bestow my fruits? And he said, this will I do: I will pull down my barns and build greater.

Luke 12:17-18

When Frank McVey first became university president, he had little desire to involve himself in the affairs of the men's athletic program. Yet in the long run, it proved to be an issue he could not avoid. His greatest complaint was always the department's lack of a structured fiscal policy. As early as 1917, he called for the department to turn over its funds to the university business agent, who would then make all necessary disbursements and publish regular financial statements. As a testimonial to the strength of athletics at the university, McVey complained for more than twenty years with few accomplishments to show for his efforts. Early, he was effectively handcuffed by pro-athletic trustees and growing alumni support. In addition, Barker's legacy (the athletic council) helped to insulate the department from unfavorable criticism. As a result, the department remained outside of his grasp and during those decades plunged deeply into debt. The expansion projects of the 1920s, most notably the new basketball arena, saddled the program with bills it could not pay—especially when the Great Depression hit. In a clear indication of McVey's limited power over sports, he succeeded in restructuring the runaway department only when it suffered the loss of student and alumni support in the late 1930s.

Before that time, however, McVey's attempts to regulate the

133

finances of athletics met with little success. McVey did manage to relieve the university from the burden of paying the salaries of the various assistant coaches, although it still funded part of the head football coach's pay. Contrary to some current opinion, the athletic department was not financially independent of the university. It did receive university assistance in this one area. For example, trustee minutes for 1920 show that Bill Juneau's salary of $2,750 was heavily funded by the university, which provided $2,400. Likewise his successor, Jack Winn, received $2,400 from the university and $2,600 from the athletic association. Other coaches of the time, Fred Murphy, Harry Gamage, and Chet Wynne, also received a $2,400 contribution from the school's general fund.[1]

In 1924, McVey did succeed in changing the nature of the head football coach's duties. Prior to that time the head coach lived in Lexington only during the season. Afterwards he returned home, usually to a northern state. The team captain or assistant coaches took care of the earliest summer practices and usually about half of the spring practice. Indicative of this arrangement, the *Kernel* noted in 1920 that Juneau would "come here from his northern home for spring practice as early as weather permits outdoor practice." He would stay approximately two weeks. Until that time, the squad would "limber up" on its own.[2] The job of head coach was essentially a part-time avocation.

McVey did not like this system, believing that the head coach should be a full-time university employee. In 1923 he succeeded in instituting his plan, which led to the resignation of Coach Jack Winn. McVey stated that the university was not dissatisfied with the performance of Winn. It merely wanted to "establish a resident, all-year-round coaching system." Winn, a Princeton graduate, refused to coach under this arrangement, stating that, with a large law practice on his hands, he "found it practically impossible to devote more than three months to football." Few people protested Winn's ousting, probably because he had managed to win only four of nine games.[3] McVey's victory did not come cheaply. The consensus of opinion among athletic council members indicated that if the coach were to work full-time, then his salary should reflect it. Consequently, new coach Fred

Murphy, a Yale product, received a substantial raise, earning $7,500 per year.[4]

For a president who believed that sports took up too much administrative time and too much university money, it would be a long twenty years. It must have seemed to the new president that at every turn he and the trustees had to debate matters relating to the athletic department's budget. As indicated earlier, McVey did not support the expenditure of large amounts of money for the new athletic arenas, believing that the university had more urgent need of the money elsewhere. The disastrous construction costs of the basketball building soon flooded the university in lawsuits.

The administration turned the matter over to the Lexington law firm of Johnston and Yancey. Senior partner J.P. Johnston reported back to the board in July 1924 that, in his opinion, most of the liens on the Basket Ball Building could not be upheld in court because the subcontractors did not file their claims in a timely manner. Typical of these subcontractors was Dayton Structural Steel, a firm that lost a great deal of money on the project. It wrote to McVey in December 1924 that it had furnished five thousand dollars' worth of steel for the basketball arena but had not been paid by the contractor. A company spokesman wrote that Dayton Steel "did not care to embarrass the university by filing a lien and, therefore, refrained from doing so, thinking that this matter would be properly straightened out in due time." The company admitted that because it did not file a lien promptly, it had no legal recourse. Yet it noted that its claim was "just as valid from a fair business point of view."[5] The administration dealt with this request in a similar manner as the others it received; it did not reply. A year later, Dayton Steel wrote again, asking for "some information as to the disposition of this matter." About a week later, McVey finally replied in a terse letter that university attorneys were looking into the matter and he could make no statement at that time.[6]

In June, Johnston reported that the Fayette Circuit Court had ruled on the first of the liens. The court directed the university to pay $9,390.90 to settle the claim of subcontractor B.D. Allen.[7] In February of the following year, the court decided the remaining cases. The presiding judge dismissed the suits of two companies while upholding the claims of ten others. In total, the court presented the university with a bill for $10,851.95. This figure did not include $372 in court costs, $193.65 in interest due to one of the claimants, or several thousand dollars the university owed to its attorneys. On February 11, the business agent turned over to Johnston the numerous checks to settle the matter.[8] Unfortunately, these legal proceedings did not actually close the books on the gymnasium saga. The athletic department soon found it difficult to pay on its loans. When the Depression hit, this problem intensified manyfold.

During such stringent times, McVey began to grow weary of the athletic department's slipshod accounting and failures to submit accurate financial statements. He requested biannual statements but received them at irregular intervals and sometimes not at all. Moreover, the statements were often incomplete, inaccurate, and contradictory. The athletic council also fell behind on its payments to the university for the stadium loan. In September 1930, McVey told the board that the council owed the school fifty-five thousand dollars. He noted that "these amounts would materially relieve the university from the financial difficulties in which it finds itself at the present time."[9] McVey asked the council to account for its inability to meet its financial obligations. He received no reply. Indeed, the council did not submit a financial statement for the 1930 football season. Angered by this refusal, McVey ordered an outside audit.

The auditing firm returned a very critical report of the athletic council's fiscal policies. It described extremely sloppy bookkeeping plagued by incomplete or missing records. For example, the department kept virtually no records of ticket sales, forcing the auditors to estimate attendance by subtracting the number of unsold tickets still on hand from the known stadium capacity. The auditors also complained that the council kept no records concerning the number of game-day programs sold or the money derived therefrom. Nor did it record any alumni or fan contributions. The audit seemed to reveal that for the athletic council, cash on hand meant quite literally that. The accountants were horrified to learn that "Daddy" Boles, athletic council treasurer, kept a large amount of cash in his desk drawers, making little or no effort to record its source or disbursement. This fact later lent credence to charges that the football team paid certain players out of a secret slush fund.[10]

The audit revealed that the athletic department had grossed $140,916.83 for the 1930 calendar year. Its biggest sources of income were as follows: football, $90,129.63; student fees, $24,703.60; basketball, $8,646.78; and the high school basketball tournament, $8,365.00. The program spent liberally as well. Recorded disbursements for the year stood at $147,761.88. The department's balance at year's beginning of $16,369.81 kept the program out of debt. Together with $4,380.71 due from the university, the department made a profit of $13,905.47. This profit existed only on paper because the athletic council applied the entire amount to various bank loans, leaving the program with a zero balance. The audit was extremely critical of the department's long-standing practice of taking out short-term loans from local banks at the beginning of the football season with the intentions of paying them off with football profits. In September of that year, for example, the department borrowed ten thousand dollars from First National Bank and Trust of Lexington in the form of a six-month note at 6 percent interest. The council had paid two thousand on the loan with the remainder due in March.[11]

The earliest years of the depression were not felt as heavily in Kentucky as in some places. In this rural state, the stock market collapse did not suddenly disrupt the economy. In fact, the enrollment at the university steadily climbed during these years, rising from 3,702 for the 1927-1928 academic year to 4,992 for 1931-1932. By December 1931, McVey claimed that UK was the third largest university in the south, trailing only Tulane and the University of Texas.[12] Yet eventually the depression and the accompanying drought caught up with the state. Spring 1932 found the university in dire straights. In March, McVey announced pay cuts. All staff earning in excess of $1,300 suffered a 10 percent cut; for persons making less, the cut was 5 percent.[13]

This cost-cutting measure did not produce the necessary savings and so, in April, McVey limited salaries to a maximum of $100 per person per month.[14] By June 1, the school ran out of money and suspended all salaries. By the end of the fiscal year, the amount of unpaid salaries totaled more than $200,000.[15] The president complimented the faculty and staff of the university for bearing this hardship "without murmur or complaint." He stated that he knew that his decisions had imposed hardships upon them. He also complimented them for their high morale, esprit de corps, and absolute loyalty.[16] At this inopportune moment, the athletic council found it difficult to secure loans from local banks and appeared before the board of trustees requesting the university to endorse a proposed loan to cover operating expenses. An incensed McVey refused, noting that the school had no authority to make such an endorsement.[17]

In fall 1932, the first signs of opposition to the football team appeared among the students. The heads of numerous fraternities and other student organizations presented a petition to the president calling for the resignation of head football coach Harry Gamage. The students also requested a reorganization of "the financial administration and personnel of this department." Any financial restructuring would, the students believed, be "conducive to a more profitable and judicious expenditure of athletic funds [and] would redound to the mutual benefit of the student body and the university and would be a move in furtherance of the athletic progress of this institution." The student council also passed a similar resolution.[18]

Gamage, an Illinois graduate, had coached the Wildcats since 1927, becoming the first coach in school history to stay more than three years in that job.[19] His biggest problem seemed to be living up to the extremely high expectations of the students and alumni. In 1929, Gamage enjoyed a sterling season, losing only to national powerhouse Alabama. The next season, the team started out 4-0, fueling euphoric talk of a Rose Bowl invitation. Unfortunately, these hopes were dashed when UK lost three of its last four games. The student yearbook hailed the season as "a success in every way except one—everybody expected too much." Not many years ago, the yearbook explained, UK fans were happy if the Wildcats beat Centre and held Alabama and Tennessee to close scores. After 1929, however, the fair-weather fans "grew rabid in their expectations," and nothing short of a conference championship would have satisfied their demands.[20]

Similar scenarios were repeated during the next several seasons. The football team roared through the first half of the season but fared very badly in the second half at the hands of stronger conference teams. From 1930 to 1933, Gamage's teams won nineteen of thirty-six games (51 percent). Kentucky's lack of success against conference rivals prompted fans on and off campus to speculate on remedies for the team's ills. A great deal of talk centered on the team's finances. Many of the Wildcat faithful believed that the university must recruit promising high school athletes throughout the South more aggressively. To do so, the school would have to find the money to provide scholarships.

Such talk greatly disturbed McVey. He told the board that the athletic council was already spending more money than it was making. This trend could not continue, especially during such lean economic times. He did not see how the struggling athletic program could possibly grant scholarships. He urged the board to form a committee to study the matter.[21] Addressing the student petition, he believed that the students meant well but were ignorant "of the organization and procedures in the case of athletic matters." He wrote in his diary that the student body, although praiseworthy in many regards, was "still adolescent."[22]

Following another disappointing season (a 5-5 record), Gamage submitted his resignation. He told the athletic council that he knew he had not been as successful as many fans had hoped. Although he offered no alibi, the *Kernel* presented several on his behalf. The paper claimed that the "coach had received much adverse criticism during the last two years when his team failed to come up to expectations due to injuries and ineligibilities."[23] Within two weeks, the fast-moving council had chosen his successor. On December 8 it announced the appointment of Chet Wynne as head football coach and athletic director. Wynne had played football at Notre Dame under fabled coach Knute Rockne. After graduation, he won two championships while coaching

"at a small Missouri school" and two more at Creighton University.
Next, he moved to Auburn, "when conditions were much worse than
they are at the university now." In 1932, he posted an unbeaten record
at Auburn. The *Kernel,* noting that Wynne's teams had always been
able to score, hoped that the new coach would bring Kentucky "out of
the football wilderness."[24] In addition to his duties as coach and athletic director, Wynne was to teach in the physical education department during the off season.[25]

Although he desperately wanted to, McVey could not escape dealing with the financial matters of the athletic council. In 1936, he told
the board that he had received another request from the council. It
asked the president to earmark federal money from the Works Progress
Administration (WPA) grants for its use. Specifically the council wanted
the WPA to fund construction of two more sections for the football
stadium, costing an estimated forty thousand dollars. McVey told the
council that he would present the matter to the board. He did so, but
urged the trustees to reject this request. He reminded the board that
the existing stadium had proven adequate for all but two recent games.
He stated that "the university would hardly be justified in such an
expenditure to meet a need of that kind." He did, however, recom-
mend using WPA funds to build a new field house that could be used
as an indoor practice facility for the football team and a welcomed
addition to the physical education department. He indicated that the
university had three gymnasiums, and, with the exception of the basketball arena, they were more or less makeshifts. The need for more
physical education space had become even more critical when a fire
heavily damaged one of the gymnasiums.[26] At the July meeting, the
trustees discussed the field house issue. Professor Terrell estimated
the cost of the building at ten thousand dollars. After much debate,
they concluded that the cost was too high, and the majority voted to
table the issue. The athletic council did, however, receive good news
relating to the WPA. In September, the WPA finished work on a new
running track and a concrete reinforced press box at McLean Stadium. The cost of the construction totaled $27,192.46, of which
$20,041.35 was paid in federal funds while the city of Lexington paid

the remainder as the project's official sponsor. No university money went into the project. McVey declared the press box and track to be the finest in the south and "a material aid in improving the facilities of the athletic field."[27] The press box was equipped for telephone, telegraph, and radio transmission. The next week, the *Kernel* announced that radio station WHAS would broadcast the first Wildcat football game.[28]

Also at that September meeting, the trustees discussed an issue that refused to die. Plans for a field house, which McVey thought sank in July, resurfaced. The president learned that since the summer trustee meeting, the athletic council had gone over his head, appealing directly to Governor Chandler. The governor favored building the field house, believing that a combination of state and federal money could pay for it.[29] The next month, the trustees approved plans for the building, estimated to cost fifty thousand dollars and paid for by state funds and a Public Works Administration (PWA) grant.[30]

McVey did not like the manner in which the original estimate of ten thousand dollars had ballooned to fifty thousand dollars. Nor did he like the athletic council's suggestion to add funds for an athletic dorm to the field house budget. Although university money was not technically committed to the project, the president still had vivid memories of the Alumni Gymnasium episode, which left the university with a considerable cleanup bill. He opposed this project, citing more critical needs on campus than new athletic facilities. In the long run, he was able to thwart the pro-athletic faction. McVey submitted a six-year plan of construction to be paid for with WPA/PWA money. As shown in table 3, he placed the athletic-related projects late in the construction schedule (so they would, perhaps, not be built) and gave top priority to academic buildings.

Despite the money pumped in by the government, the athletic program still struggled mightily to sustain itself. Its budget statement for September 30, 1935, revealed that it began the football season with a meager balance of $183.89. Somehow, the athletic council had to come up with $18,975 to pay on its loans before November. It could not. A year later, the department budget showed red ink for the first

TABLE 3
Proposed Public Works Construction Projects
at the University of Kentucky, 1937-1942

1937	
student union building	$200,000
law building	$75,000
engineering lab	$50,000
cooperative home for women	$50,000
1938	
home economics building	$100,000
science labs	$250,000
art building	$75,000
women's dormitory	$100,000
1939	
fine arts building	$200,000
college of arts	$200,000
chemistry building addition	$75,000
bachelor hall	$150,000
education building addition	$50,000
1940	
women's gymnasium	$200,000
administration building	$150,000
men's dormitory	$150,000
field house/natatorium	$150,000
1941	
museum	$150,000
armory	$170,000
communications building	$200,000
physics building	$150,000
1942	
athletic dorm	$100,000
science building addition	$100,000
stadium addition	$50,000
engineering building	$50,000
library addition	$300,000

Source: University of Kentucky Board of Trustees Minutes, 14
October 1936, 28-29. Special Collections, M.I. King Library
North, University of Kentucky, Lexington.

time. The $3,500 in unpaid bills listed did not include the nearly $8,000 that had been due in September to First National Bank and Trust.[31]

McVey told the board that he doubted if Kentucky could compete successfully in the Southeastern Conference. He noted that the university was on the periphery of the conference geographically, and apparently financially as well. It must also be considered, he continued, that conference schools had recently adopted "a rather frank policy for the subsidizing of athletes" through scholarships. The president did not see how UK could do likewise. Already, the athletic program found itself in deep financial difficulties. Perhaps the board should consider whether in the long run it would be advisable for the school to withdraw from the conference.[32]

For more than a decade McVey tried to curtail what he saw as reckless spending on the part of the athletic council. Yet during that time he failed to instill any sense of fiscal stability. The council, buoyed by the support of the alumni, the trustees, and the governor, seemed immune to his criticisms. By the late 1930s, however, tiny fissures were beginning to appear in that support. Chet Wynne, counted on to duplicate the success of his basketball counterpart and bring the school to prominence in the conference, was only winning about half of his games. Soon rumblings of discontent sounded from across the state, and those cracks grew into gaping holes in the popularity of Wynne and the athletic council. Only then could McVey hope to initiate long-needed reform. A disappointing football season in 1937 gave him that opportunity.

THE PURGE
OF 1938

But God said unto him, thou fool, this night thy soul shall be required of thee.

Luke 12:20

THE 1937 FOOTBALL SEASON opened on a very ominous note. Before summer practice began, President McVey summoned Coach Wynne into his office and asked for his resignation. During this brief meeting, McVey tried to address the rampant rumors that Wynne's drinking problem had become a public embarrassment and a hindrance to his coaching. McVey reminded him that in January (at the time of Wynne's contract extension), he had promised that the president "need have no anxiety about his conduct." Since that time, however, McVey claimed that the coach had broken his word. Furthermore, he did not think that Wynne could go through the entire fall "without another let down." McVey thought that a resignation would be the best way to "help the man and protect the university."[1]

Wynne refused McVey's request, telling the president that only politicians resigned. Once again he promised that there would be "no occasion for any action." At that time, Wynne launched into a rather ill-advised argument with McVey. He complained that his job was made unnecessarily difficult because of the university's failure to provide more money to the athletic department. Without sufficient scholarship money, a new field house, and an athletic dorm, Wynne believed that he could not compete in the Southeastern Conference. Plagued for more than a decade by the athletic department's fiscal woes, McVey was not receptive to these complaints. The meeting ended and McVey

Football coach and athletic director Chet Wynne

did not pursue the matter of Wynne's resignation further. During such hard economic times, he did not relish the thought of having to buy out the three years remaining on Wynne's contract.[2]

When the season began, Wynne's standing with the administration, the student body, the team, and the alumni began to deteriorate sharply. The *Kernel* stated that to venture a prediction of a victory-studded season after watching Wynne conduct drills would be "raw madness."[3] The student publication criticized the team at every juncture, calling it unimpressive, dreary, and totally outclassed. There was more than a grain of truth in the *Kernel* attacks. The Wildcats managed to win four games but lost six, including all conference games. Making matters worse, the team's six losses all came in the form of shutouts. UK thus became the only SEC team not to score against a conference foe.[4]

Making matters worse, the team lost heavily at the turnstiles as well. In the words of the *Kernel*, the team (with the exception of the Tennessee game) often played to many "vacant pews." Fans indeed stayed away from McLean Stadium in droves, leaving the program with "red ink splattered here and there on the books."[5] Assessing the matter, McVey told the trustees that the football team had earned only fourteen thousand dollars during the season. This amount compared very badly with previous earnings: thirty-one thousand dollars in 1936 and thirty-five thousand dollars in 1935. Football's profitability was crucial to the entire athletic department because it generated most of the money needed for the whole year. McVey calculated that the entire athletic program lost approximately seventeen thousand dollars that fall, forcing the university "to take over the obligations of the department for the rest of the year." He further noted that this situation greatly embarrassed him in the light of budgetary constraints already faced by the university.[6]

McVey may well have been planning some corrective measures, but before he could act, the team itself took action. Events of December and January provoked a dramatic player revolt. After the season, two popular coaches, Tom Gorman and Porter Grant, resigned. The players mistakenly believed that they had been forced out. Led by newly elected team captain Sherman Hinkebein, the players presented a petition to McVey in early January. The petition began, "we the undersigned football representatives of the State University (not the University of Lexington) hereby formally and vigorously protest the resignation of assistant coaches Porter Grant and Thomas Gorman." The players threatened to quit if the department did not rehire the two coaches.[7]

The athletic council tried to dispel the notion that the coaches had been compelled to resign. According to Professor Funkhouser of the athletic council, Gorman had asked for a raise and a longer contract but the council refused, citing the disastrous season and resulting lack of funds. Unhappy with his salary and the lack of security that accompanied the one-year contract, he decided to put his law degree to work and moved to Chicago where he hoped to pass the bar exam and work in the district attorney's office. Grant, on the other hand, left UK to take a coaching position at Auburn. A *Herald* reporter phoned Grant to confirm this claim.[8]

With this issue settled, the players began a lengthy criticism of the athletic council, claiming that it did not represent the entire state. According to the athletes, the council should include one member from every section of the state. This plan limited Lexington to one representative while giving an equal voice to Louisville, Ashland, Paducah, Middlesboro, Pineville, and Covington. McVey replied that SEC rules required the faculty to hold the majority on the council. The players then requested that the university retain Wynne and reaffirmed their willingness to strike if the makeup of the council were not changed.[9]

This was the opportunity for which McVey had long waited. Emboldened by the players' revolt and alumni rumblings, he suggested that the university form a committee to consider a reorganization of the athletic council. McVey succeeded in bypassing the council by assembling a five-member committee that included McVey (representing the administration), arts and sciences dean Paul Boyd (representing the faculty), Doc Rodes of the alumni association, and David Pettus, president of the student council. The new committee would examine the entire athletic structure, including the council, coaches, and all concerned. As the *Herald* indicated, "some action was expected after the disastrous football season."[10]

By harnessing alumni discontent across the state, McVey succeeded in restructuring the athletic department without it seeming to be a personal attack on his part. The reorganization committee planned to meet with alumni chapters all over the state, listening to their complaints and suggestions. This process lasted for one month and led many UK faithful to speculate on its outcome. One Associated Press writer predicted that any reorganization would be very mild. As he described, there was nothing wrong with the organization of the athletic department; it was only experiencing a temporary money problem. He noted that like any business, UK athletics had to outbid its competitors. The fans could not blame high school stars for going to other SEC teams that offered them more money. After all, he scolded, "you can't pay bills with school spirit and you can't build a Rose Bowl team on ethics." The program's difficulties would cease as soon as the alumni and local business men took a more active role in raising money.[11]

This writer underestimated the level of dissatisfaction throughout the state. Over the course of the next month, suggestions for reforming the athletic program poured in to the reorganization committee. Shortly after the formation of the committee, the football players presented another plan for change. This plan confused many observers, especially the *Herald,* because it was an "abrupt about face" from the team's first proposal. The new plan called for Wynne's resignation and the appointment of an athletic director who would not divide his duties by coaching. In a clear reversal of the previous team submission, the new proposal limited the alumni to one representative on the athletic council, which would include McVey, four faculty members, and two students. The newspaper hinted that McVey particularly liked this plan for reorganization.[12] This submission drew a prompt and heated response from numerous football players who indicated that it did not represent the wishes of the entire team. Unidentified team members stated that it had been presented by three players only (most notably Hinkebein), advised by several faculty members. The *Herald* identified the faculty involved as Bernie Shively, Dan Terrell, and James Shropshire. Several athletes were outraged that this splinter group had taken it upon themselves to contradict their original demands.[13]

In quick succession, individual alumni and organized alumni chapters voiced their opinions on the matter. Among the first to do so was Wallace Muir, a prominent Lexington figure and key member of both the alumni association and the athletic council. He had played football for UK and the Lexington Athletic Club in the 1890s, as well as trying his hand at coaching during that same decade.[14] Muir criticized the university for not investing more money in the sports program, claiming that other SEC schools spent hundreds of thousands of dollars on stadiums, salaries, and scholarships while the UK administration provided no financial assistance (not exactly true) to its athletic program. Muir suggested that the university provide free room and board (in a separate athletic dorm) for ninety athletes, as well as twenty-five thousand dollars for the yearly salaries of all coaches.[15] Quite literally, Muir thought that the university should either "put up or shut up." He wrote to athletic council chairman M.E. Ligon that the university in his opinion had three choices: spend enough money to compete with SEC schools, take defeat without complaint, or withdraw from the conference and compete with schools on the same financial level. Ligon passed this letter on to McVey.[16]

Muir also criticized the university's admission policies for being too strict. He believed that requiring incoming freshmen to have high school credits in algebra and geometry hurt the football team's ability to recruit in the region. Every year, he claimed, athletes denied admission to UK went to other schools in the conference where admission standards were lower. He also proposed eliminating the athletic council entirely and investing all authority in a full-time athletic director. Finally, he suggested that the school schedule more popular non-conference opponents in order to boost attendance and gate receipts. He believed that the Wildcat football team should schedule at least one game each year with the University of Louisville. In a rare editorial, the *Herald* endorsed Muir's plan.[17]

The reorganization committee encouraged local alumni chapters to speak out on the subject. Committee members attended chapter meetings in Louisville, Paducah, Pineville, Ashland, Covington, and Lexington. Across the state, animosity toward Coach Wynne ran very high. Without exception, all local chapters called for his immediate resignation as head football coach and athletic director. The Louisville and the western Kentucky alumni chapters endorsed the second players' plan. Both were very vocal about keeping Coach Rupp, whose contract expired that spring. The Boyd County alumni chapter, on the other hand, favored a modified version of the first players' proposal, believing that Lexington had too much influence on athletic policy. To remedy that situation, it believed that one representative from each state congressional district should sit on the athletic council.[18]

The Lexington chapter was the last to meet. It too strongly condemned Wynne's performance, claiming that he had failed in his duties as head coach and athletic director and should be dismissed immediately without compensation for his remaining contract period. The chapter believed that the athletic council should be stripped of all decision-making power. By SEC rules, it could not be abolished but it could be relegated to an advisory board, as was the case at the University of Alabama. The chapter believed that the university should underwrite all athletic salaries, provide an athletic dorm, and give Adolph Rupp a substantial raise. The members reserved their strongest criticism for the haphazard manner in which the department distributed scholarship money. This system, more of a slush fund than a scholarship program, drew heated attacks from the Lexington alumni. They wholeheartedly condemned paying some players cash while others received none. According to their information, twelve Wildcats had received money in varying amounts during the previous season. All revenues of the department, the alumni believed, should be received, deposited, and disbursed by the university business office with careful attention to up-to-date audits.[19]

While the various alumni groups debated the issue of reorganization, President McVey sought the advice of trusted friends and colleagues. M.E. Potter, a UK professor for twelve years who now taught at Louisiana State University, wrote that in his opinion the UK athletic council had too much power and insulated the athletic department from the administration. He believed that it should be stripped of all decision-making power. An athletic director appointed by and answerable to the university president should run the program. Potter sharply criticized the athletic department for following "a policy of aloofness and an attitude of superiority" rather than trying to foster goodwill among fans and alumni. Thus far it appeared to Potter that the only action taken by the department concerning its financial difficulties had been to "bellyache about the declining crowds." The department, he felt, must realize the crucial importance of gate receipts. Accordingly, "whoever had the responsibility of running the department had to be something of a promoter." Potter also suggested that the council should free the basketball coach from the added burdens of coaching other sports.[20]

In a similar letter to Paul Boyd, Potter wrote that under no circumstances should the department allow fans or alumni to give money directly to the players. All donations and gate receipts must go into a general fund and be disbursed to meet the needs of the department.

As Potter explained, "if one athlete gets five dollars a week from some interested supporter, another ten, and perhaps several others nothing, herein is a great chance for dissatisfaction among the athletes."[21]

McVey suffered no shortage of advice. He categorized the suggestions and preserved them with his official papers. Many of the proposals came from anonymous sources. A great many of them criticized the performances of S.A. Boles, Wallace Muir, and Chet Wynne. Several potentially helpful fans complained that for years Boles had invited a number of high school athletes to play for UK with the pledge of financial aid. Frequently, when the athlete arrived on campus, the promise of a scholarship had vanished. Another advice-giver alleged that Wallace Muir operated a slush fund, doling out money to some athletes but denying it to others. This person claimed that Muir had "things so in his clutches" that it was surprising that he had not completely strangled the whole program.[22]

Many writers condemned the actions of Wynne, whom they depicted as a drunk. Numerous people claimed that Wynne had appeared intoxicated, especially at games, and had lost the respect of his players and team supporters. Additionally, Wynne's alleged drinking had been a bad influence on the players, encouraging them to break training. Some people blamed alcohol for Wynne's infuriating habit of accepting speaking engagements at high school and alumni banquets and then failing to appear. Finally, one Wildcat fan wrote that the department should give scholarship preference "to Southern boys having the spirit of Lee and the fight of Jackson." Similarly, the university should end its established habit of bringing in coaches from northern schools and instead hire southerners.[23]

As the review process wore on, speculations about its outcome increased. On February 18, the *Herald* reported that the reorganization committee had met the previous evening to finalize its recommendations to the administration. Although neither McVey nor any committee member would confirm or deny anything, the *Herald* claimed that it "had it on good authority" that Chet Wynne's resignation was imminent. Adding fuel to the abundant rumors, the paper noted that Adolph Rupp had been summoned to the meeting. His stay was short, and he made no comment on the meeting.[24] The next day, McVey officially announced the committee's findings. The plan, which still needed trustee approval, called for a dilution of the athletic council's power. Henceforward, it would serve only in an advisory capacity. Under the new arrangement it included the president, three faculty members (two less than before), two students, and the president of the alumni association. Previously, three alumni had served on the council. The committee invested all decision-making power in an athletic director who answered only to the university president. Contrary to the opinions expressed by some alumni earlier, the plan did not prohibit the athletic director from coaching.[25]

The new departmental framework required that all money from sports be paid into the business office and paid out on requisition of the director and approved by the president. In addition, the department must prepare an annual budget to be approved in the same manner as all other university budgets. Once a year, the athletic director would order an audit and publish its findings.[26] Concerning salaries, the *Kernel* wrote that "the huge salaries of bygone days were no more." Head coaches were to be given the rank and salary of professors, while assistant coaches would have the rank and salary of assistant professors. Coach Wynne submitted his resignation, but McVey made no comment on the terms of his contract settlement. It was widely rumored that Governor Chandler earmarked state funds to buy out the two remaining years of Wynne's contract.[27]

The next task involved choosing an athletic director. To that end McVey appointed another committee, which included Pettus and Rodes from the reorganization committee and two faculty members. This body would make a nonbinding recommendation to McVey, who in turn would present his nominee to the board for final approval. The *Herald* believed that the overwhelming choice for the position was Adolph Rupp and printed a photograph of the basketball coach under the article's headline. A few days later, the *Herald* announced the committee's recommendation, which was approved by McVey. It was not Rupp, but instead Bernie Shively, head of the physical education department and former line coach under Harry Gamage. Shively's first

Albert D. "Ab" Kirwan, 1925 football team captain and All-Conference running back. He later served the university as head football coach, dean of men, professor of history, and president.

decision as athletic director was to name Ab Kirwan, star running back and 1925 team captain, as head football coach. For the past several years, Kirwan had coached at Louisville Manual High School. Shively's second action extended the contract of Rupp. The *Herald* quoted Shively as saying that he had "the utmost respect for Coach Rupp and his ability to build winning basketball teams. His record speaks for itself." Rupp later claimed that he had been offered the athletic director's position but turned it down. He stated that he feared that if he could not win football games as athletic director, he might lose his job as basketball coach.[28] McVey did not like Shively's decision to retain S.A. "Daddy" Boles to manage ticket sales, but made no open protest and the board approved all of the appointments.[29]

Almost immediately, Shively and Kirwan embarked upon a speaking tour of the state. Occasionally accompanied by Adolph Rupp, they targeted alumni chapters, speaking at many alumni banquets across the commonwealth. Shively desperately wanted to smooth over the antagonistic behavior of Wynne, the 1937 season, and the reorganization purge as well. At each of his stops, Shively suggested that Wildcat fans should form booster clubs not strictly limited to university alumni. For a ten-dollar membership fee, a booster could receive priority status in purchasing tickets. For his part, Kirwan tried to preach patience at these gatherings. He warned the alumni that building a successful team took a great deal of time. He urged them not to expect too much too soon.[30] Kirwan's words were quite prophetic. The 1938 edition of Blue and White football suffered through the worst season in more than forty years. After opening with wins against Maryville and Oglethorpe, the team composed mostly of inexperienced sophomores lost the next seven games: many by shutouts. Attendance, however, was up substantially over the previous year. The *Kernel* estimated that twelve thousand fans watched the game against Washington and Lee and a similar number saw the Wildcats play Xavier. Larger crowds filed into McLean Stadium to see the home team lose to such noted foes as Alabama and Vanderbilt.[31]

Despite its abysmal win-loss record, the football team appeared to have won a major victory that fall. After losing a great deal of fan support and suffering both a player and an alumni revolt, the program succeeded in winning many of them back. The reorganization pacified McVey, appeased the players, and gave hope to the alumni and other supporters. So too did the 1939 season, which saw Kirwan's squad post a 6-2-1 record. Best of all, the Wildcats that year beat SEC rival Georgia, tied Alabama, and registered its first win against Vanderbilt since that series began forty-three years earlier.[32] Still unanswered, however, were the many financial questions that plagued the athletic department. It would take much longer than a few weeks to reorganize the program's chaotic financial condition.

EPILOGUE

ALTHOUGH IT IS MORE than a little ironic, a good case could be made that many of the problems of the football team were caused by the basketball team. On one hand, the cost overruns and legal expenses of the Alumni Gymnasium project undoubtedly weakened the budget of the entire athletic program and poisoned its relationship with the administration. More directly, the success of the basketball team created a higher level of fan expectation. Chet Wynne won about 57 percent of his games in his stay at Kentucky, but compared to Adolph Rupp's 82 percent mark, it was not good enough. Furthermore, Wynne's inability to win games in the conference contrasted sharply with Rupp's thrilling tournament championships. This contrast was sharpened because the decline of football corresponded neatly with the rise of basketball. On a positive note, one could argue that Rupp's success may have been the only factor that kept the university in the Southeastern Conference. Had it not been for basketball's tournament championships, McVey might well have convinced the board that the school should withdraw from the conference because of the football team's inability to compete against major SEC powers.

The athletic department's financial problems continued and in fact outlasted President McVey. In June 1939, he informed the trustees that on November 10 he would reach the compulsory retirement age of seventy. The board granted the president an extension until July 1, 1940. McVey served the university for twenty-three years and saw it develop, mature, and expand into a true university. Yet the depression dashed many of his hopes and goals. He had wanted a larger library, a

156

medical college, a stronger graduate program, and more laboratory space for the engineering department. He also believed that the school needed an updated physical plant. As it was, the campus operated nine separate heating plants, which were costly, inefficient, unreliable, and, as shown by the gymnasium fire, dangerous. To close friends, he revealed that his failure to achieve these goals because of the depression upset him greatly. He also bitterly complained that he had spent so much time on athletic squabbles when far more important matters needed his attention.[1]

Not long after McVey's retirement, the newly reorganized athletic department saw its first personnel change. In 1945, football coach Ab Kirwan took a leave of absence to attend Duke University and work on a doctorate.[2] He returned to UK two years later, not as the football coach but rather as dean of men (a title later changed to dean of students) and professor of history. In 1968, he became university president, serving one year.

The athletic department's finances improved slowly. Its 1940 budget showed a modest ten-thousand-dollar profit, which it applied to old loans. It paid the interest and five hundred dollars on the principle of its nearly seventeen-year-old Basket Ball Building loan and renewed the balance yet again.[3] Any additional building projects had to wait until after World War II. Consequently, the basketball team continued to play in the cramped quarters of Alumni Gymnasium while the football team still played in what was essentially half of a stadium. In 1948, the board of trustees approved plans for the expansion of McLean Stadium. Construction continued over the years as funds allowed.[4] By the early 1970s, the stadium's seating capacity had increased to 37,500. In August 1974, wrecking crews tore it down. In its place, the university built a fine arts center. With the money from a successful fund-raising drive, the university then built Commonwealth Stadium in its current location.[5] The basketball program eventually moved to the more spacious Memorial Coliseum and eventually to the cavernous Rupp Arena.

On the University of Kentucky campus, there are abundant reminders of this period. As the university built over the years, it honored its early leaders by naming new buildings in their memory. The honorees mentioned in this work include James Patterson, A.M. Miller, James White, Henry Barker, Sara Blanding, Frank McVey, Ab Kirwan, Bernie Shively, W.D. Funkhouser, A.B. "Happy" Chandler, and Adolph Rupp.[6] An often overlooked plaque marks the spot of the original Stoll Field.

After the period studied here, the athletic department ran afoul of the administration as well as the various governing bodies with some degree of regularity. Other UK presidents complained that athletic scandals took up too much of their time and tarnished the image of the university. Yet never again were there calls to abolish the program. Never again did it experience such a total shake-up. Having survived its primitive days and its many brushes with disaster, collapse, and sanction, it became one of the finest, most successful, and most visible college athletic programs in the nation. It would be priceless to hear what Frank McVey would say about the millions of dollars earned annually by the university's sports teams. Perhaps he would smile to learn that the athletic department recently made a large donation to the university's Commonwealth Library project.

□

NOTES

1. "Central Wins in Miller Case," *Lexington Herald,* 7 October 1908, 3.

2. University of Kentucky Board of Trustees (BOT) Minutes, 4 June 1902, 124-25, Special Collections, M.I. King Library North, University of Kentucky, Lexington, Kentucky.

3. For information on Patterson's early years, see James F. Hopkins, *The University of Kentucky: Origins and Early Years* (Lexington: Univ. of Kentucky Press, 1951), 136-37.

4. "Strict Rules Made in New Conference," *Herald,* 1 March 1924, 4; "SIC Meeting Opens Tonight," *Herald,* 8 December 1927, 1; "SIAA Standings," *Herald,* 20 November 1933, 6; "Varsity Basketball," University of Kentucky Student Yearbook, *Kentuckian,* 1933, 166, Special Collections, M.I. King Library North, University of Kentucky, Lexington, Kentucky.

INTRODUCTION

1. BOT Minutes, 11 December 1906, 113.

2. For an analysis of faculty committees at other schools, see Ronald A. Smith, *Sports and Freedom: The Rise of Big-Time College Athletics* (New York: Oxford Univ. Press, 1988), 124-31.

3. Robin Lester, *Stagg's University: The Rise, Decline, and Fall of Big-Time Football at Chicago* (Urbana: Univ. of Illinois Press, 1995); for a brief description

of Hutchins's 1939 action, see Alexander Wolff, "Broken Beyond Repair," *Sports Illustrated,* 12 June 1995, 20-22.

4. "A Football Diploma," *Herald,* 27 November 1897, 7.

5. Cited in Helen Deiss Irvin, *Hail Kentucky! A Pictorial History of the University of Kentucky* (Lexington: Univ. of Kentucky Press, 1965), 29.

6. "Navy Football Player with Broken Neck Has a Chance," *Herald,* 1 November 1909, 1; "Three Recent Victims of Collegiate Football," *Herald,* 21 November 1909, 1; "Nineteen Football Fatalities So Far," *Herald,* 23 November 1910, 5.

7. "Gridiron Hero is Dying," *Herald,* 25 October 1909, 3.

8. "Leg is Broken in Six Places," *Herald,* 15 October 1906, 2.

9. BOT Minutes, 24 February 1931, 9-12.

ONE: The Arrival of Football on Campus

1. BOT Minutes, 11 December 1895, 55.

2. Smith, *Sports and Freedom,* 67-77.

3. *Kernel,* 26 September 1924, Special Collections, M.I. King Library North, University of Kentucky, Lexington, Kentucky.

4. Russell Rice, *The Wildcats: A Story of Kentucky Football* (Huntsville, Ala.: Strode, 1975), 11-14. In 1876, Harvard, Yale, and Princeton adopted a rugby-style format. By the 1890s, it had supplanted the soccer style in the rest of the country, see Smith, *Sports and Freedom,* 76, 83.

5. Hopkins, *University of Kentucky,* 181.

6. University of Kentucky Student Yearbook, *Memoria,* 1894, 78, Special Collections, M.I. King Library North, University of Kentucky, Lexington, Kentucky.

7. Ibid. See also Richard Charles Stoll Biographical File, Special Collections, M.I. King Library North, University of Kentucky, Lexington, Kentucky.

8. *Memoria,* 1894, 78. See also Rice, *Wildcats,* 22.

9. *Memoria,* 1894, 78. See also Carl B. Cone, *The University of Kentucky: A Pictorial History* (Lexington: Univ. Press of Kentucky, 1988).

10. Smith, *Sports and Freedom,* 119.

11. Ibid., 122, 160; "State College Defeated," *Herald,* 27 November 1896, 8; "Easy Victory for State College," *Herald,* 24 October 1897, 2.

12. BOT Minutes, 31 May 1893, 110; 6 June 1894, 129-30.

13. BOT Minutes, 6 June 1894, 126; 11 December 1894, 164.

14. Hopkins, *University of Kentucky,* 184.

15. Ibid., 159-60, 192; BOT Minutes, 9 December 1896, 97-98.

16. Hopkins, *University of Kentucky,* 143, 153.

17. Ibid.

18. Mabel Pollitt, *A Biography of James Kennedy Patterson, President of the University of Kentucky from 1869-1910* (Louisville: Westerfield-Bonte, 1925), 188.

19. BOT Minutes, 11 December 1895, 55.

20. BOT Minutes, 3 June 1896, 74-75.

21. BOT Minutes, 4 June 1896, 87-88. For a description of the grading/merit/demerit scale, see BOT Minutes, 31 July 1895, 37.

22. Hopkins, *University of Kentucky,* 167.

23. BOT Minutes, December 1894, 164; 11 December 1901, 75-76.

24. BOT Minutes, 1 June 1898, 182; 9 December 1902, 164-65.

25. Cited in Smith, *Sports and Freedom,* 121. Quote is dated 1882.

26. BOT Minutes, 1 June 1898, 182; 9 December 1902, 164-65; 1 June 1909, 8-9.

27. Cited in Hopkins, *University of Kentucky,* 166-67.

28. "Big Game Off," *Herald,* 1 December 1897, 8; "KU Boys Home Again," *Lexington Leader,* 8 October 1898, 7.

29. "LAC Defeated," *Herald,* 18 October 1896, 12; "Easy Victory for State College," *Herald,* 24 October 1897, 2; "Whipped," *Herald,* 26 November 1897, 2.

30. "First Game," *Herald,* 3 October 1897, 8; "Game Broke Up in a Row," *Leader,* 13 November 1898, 2.

31. "State College Boys Win," *Leader,* 2 October 1898, 6; "LAC Defeated," *Herald,* 18 October 1896, 12.

32. "Centre Victorious," *Herald,* 27 September 1897, 8.

33. "Football," *Herald,* 27 September 1897, 8; "KU and SC Meet on the Gridiron Here This Afternoon," *Herald,* 2 October 1897, 8.

34. "State College Football Team Will Fill All Dates, Practice Resumed," *Herald,* 20 October 1897, 5; "State College and Georgetown Play Here Tomorrow," *Herald,* 22 October 1897, 5; "Easy Victory for State College in Yesterday's Game," *Herald,* 24 October 1897.

35. Richard Charles Stoll Biographical File.

36. BOT Minutes, 1 June 1898, 197-98.

37. "State College Boys Win," *Leader,* 2 October 1898, 6.

38. Ibid.

39. "Easy for the State College 11," *Leader,* 9 October 1898, 8.

40. "State College Boys Winners," *Leader,* 30 October 1898, 2.

41. Ibid.

42. "Record Still Clean," *Leader,* 13 November 1898, 2; "Champs Are What They Look Like Now," *Leader,* 20 November 1898, 2.

43 "It Saved Old Centre," *Leader,* 16 November 1898, 5; "Centre College Has Backed Down," *Leader,* 19 November 1898, 3.

44. "No Game on Turkey Day," *Leader,* 23 November 1898, 3.

45. "State College Team Claims Championship," *Leader,* 24 November 1898, 1.

46. Cone, *University of Kentucky.* 32.

47. Ibid.; "Victorious State College 11," *Leader,* 25 November 1898, 4.

TWO: The First Athletic Scandal

1. Cited in "A Football Diploma," *Herald,* 27 November 1897, 7.

2. *Kentuckian,* 1901.

3. "State College Boys Win," *Leader,* 2 October 1898, 6.

4. Smith, *Sports and Freedom,* 8.

5. "Athletics at KSC," *Kentuckian,* 1901.

6. BOT Minutes, 2 June 1903, 194-95.

7. "Football Ambition," *Herald,* 1 November 1903, 4.

8. "Will Game Be Played?" *Herald,* 18 November 1903, 1.

9. Ibid.

10. Ibid.; University of Kentucky Student Yearbook, *Echoes,* 1904, 77.

11. Ibid.

12. Ibid.

13. "Game Between SC and KU Will Be Played Thanksgiving Day," *Herald,* 20 November 1903, 4.

14. "Football," *Herald,* 1 November 1903, 1; "Town Talk is Exclusively of Game," *Herald,* 24 November 1903, 8; "Mayor Duncan Assigns Twenty-Five Policemen," *Herald,* 25 November 1903, 1.

15. "Officials Selected," *Herald,* 24 November 1903, 1.

16. "Mayor Duncan Assigns Twenty-Five Policemen," *Herald,* 25 November 1903, 1.

17. "Crimsons Won With a Straight Team Over the Blue and White," *Herald,* 27 November 1903, 1.

18. "Records of Kentucky Elevens," *Herald,* 29 November 1903, 4.

19. *Echoes,* 1904, 71.

20. Ibid.

21. BOT Minutes, 16 June 1904, 268-69.

22. "Betting on the Big Game," *Herald,* 14 November 1904, 4.

23. "Team Eats at Training Board," *Herald,* 10 November 1904, 4.

24. "Lists are Submitted," *Herald,* 15 November 1904, 4.

25. "Lists are Passed Upon," *Herald,* 16 November 1904, 8.

26. "Shut Up and Play Ball," *Herald,* 21 November 1904, 4.

27. "Protests Erased From the Slate," *Herald,* 22 November 1904, 7.

28. "Champions Three Years Outplayed," *Herald,* 25 November 1904, 1.

29. "Awful Drubbing for State College," *Herald,* 19 November 1905, 4.

30. "State's List is Made Public," *Herald,* 16 November 1905, 5; "To Play or Not to Play, That is the Question," *Herald,* 23 November 1905, 5.

31. "To Play or Not to Play, That is the Question," *Herald,* 23 November 1905, 5.

32. "Deadlock Over Choice of Field is New Difficulty," *Herald,* 24 November 1905, 1.

33. "State College Calls Off Negotiations," *Herald,* 25 November 1905, 8.

34. "Want Teams to Get Together," *Herald,* 26 November 1905, 5.

35. "May Reach an Agreement," *Herald,* 27 November 1905, 4.

36. "College Deans Involved in Controversy," *Herald,* 28 November 1905, 1.

37. "To Play or Not to Play," *Herald,* 23 November 1905, 5.

38. "College Deans Involved in Controversy," *Herald,* 28 November 1905, 1.

39. "Sharp Exchange of Charges Ends Negotiations," *Herald,* 28 November 1905, 1.

40. "Have Clean Football or None," *Herald,* 28 November 1905, 2.

41. "KU Will Play Ohio Wesleyan," *Herald,* 29 November 1905, 4; "Crimson Team to Play Battle of the Year Today," *Herald,* 30 November 1905, 1.

42. "Crimson Team Closes Season Still Unbeaten," *Herald,* 1 December 1905, 1.

43. *Kentuckian,* 1906, 120.

44. Smith, *Sports and Freedom,* 183.

45. *Kentuckian,* 1906, 120.

46. BOT Minutes, 2 December 1905, 51-42.

47. "Town Talk is Exclusively of Game," *Herald,* 24 November 1903, 8.

48. BOT Minutes, 6 June 1906, 76-77.

49. Ibid.

50. BOT Minutes, 11 December 1906, 113.

51. BOT Minutes, 12 December 1906, 132.

52. BOT Minutes, 5 June 1907, 149-50.

53. Ibid., 155.

54. Ibid.

55. Smith, *Sports and Freedom,* 181.

56. Ibid., 95.

57. George Beard, *American Nervousness: Its Causes and Consequences* (1881; rpt., New York: Arno, 1972), 137-38.

58. William Z. Ripley, *The Races of Europe: A Sociological Study* (New York: Appleton, 1899).

59. William Castle, *Heredity and Eugenics* (Chicago: Univ. of Chicago Press, 1912), 43, 80; see also Madison Grant, *The Passing of the Great Race: The Racial Basis of European History* (New York: Charles Scribner's Sons, 1916).

60. Theodore Roosevelt, "The Law of Civilization and Decay," *Forum* (January 1897): 586-89.

61. Smith, *Sports and Freedom*, 96.

62. "Will Game Be Played?" *Herald*, 8 November 1903, 1.

63. *Kentuckian*, 1910, dedication page.

64. BOT Minutes, 14 December 1910, 138.

THREE: A Brief Moment in the Sun

1. University of Kentucky Student Newspaper, *Idea*, 2 December 1909, 8, Special Collections, M.I. King Library North, University of Kentucky, Lexington, Kentucky.

2. "May Be Football Game This Year," *Herald*, 9 September 1906, 8; "May Be An Athletic Club Organized Here," *Herald*, 12 September 1906, 6; "KU May Yet Have a Team This Year," *Herald*, 23 September 1906, 3; "No Football This Year at University," *Herald*, 9 October 1906.

3. "State College Football Team Organizes," *Herald*, 15 September 1906, 3; "Guyn-Watson," wedding announcement, *Herald*, 20 September 1906; "Football," University of Kentucky Yearbook, *Kentuckian*, 1907, 106.

4. "Central to Play Football," *Herald*, 11 October 1906, 6.

5. "First Football of the Season Today," *Herald*, 3 October 1906, 3; "Eminence Defeated by State College," *Herald*, 14 October 1906; "Leg Broken in Six Places," *Herald*, 15 October 1906, 2.

6. "Hotly Contested Game on Local Gridiron," *Herald*, 28 October 1906, 7; "Three Fatally Hurt in Football Game," *Herald*, 1 October 1906.

7. "Lexington Again Has Gone Football Mad," *Herald*, 27 November 1906, 5; "Interest in Football Game More Intense," *Herald*, 28 November 1906, 5; "Championship of Kentucky Will Be Fought Out Today," *Herald*, 29 November 1906, 1.

8. "Yelling Thousands Fill the Streets," *Herald*, 30 November 1906, 1.

9. "State Will Play Against Hanover College," *Herald*, 25 October 1907, 3.

10. "State College Teams Have a Good Supper," *Herald*, 25 October 1907, 3.

11. "Varsity Wins by 40-0 Score," *Herald*, 6 October 1907, 8.

12. "Hogan Yancey to Coach KU Team," *Herald*, 16 September 1907, 5; "KU Defeats Central University, Tying State," *Herald*, 17 November 1907, 1.

13. "Football Team May Go On Strike," *Herald*, 21 November 1907, 10.

14. "KU-State Game Postponed," *Herald*, 24 November 1907, 3.

15. "Blue and White Wins From Crimson by Score of 5-0," *Herald*, 6 December 1907, 1.

16. "Outlook for Football at State," *Herald*, 22 September 1908, 4.

17. "State University Loses to Michigan," *Herald*, 8 November 1908, 8.

18. "State University Prepares For Game," *Herald*, 7 October 1908, 10.

19. "Want College Teams to Play Football," *Herald*, 20 October 1908, 3.

20. "Local Athletes Discussed by Records," *Herald*, 8 November 1908, 8.

21. "Teams Preparing for Grim Struggle," *Herald*, 8 October 1908, 4; "Athletic Field is Named for Mr. Stoll," *Herald*, 8 October 1908, 4; "State University Wins Kentucky Championship," *Herald*, 27 November 1908, 1.

22. "E.R. Sweetland Resigns," *Kentuckian*, 1911, 153; "Sweetland Resigns," *Idea*, 8 December 1910, 1.

23. "State University Has Star Eleven," *Herald*, 19 September 1909, 4; "E.R. Sweetland," *Kentuckian*, 1910, 232.

24. "State University Football, Eleven," *Herald*, 8 October 1909, 9.

25. "Kentucky State Vanquished University of Illinois Eleven in Hard Fought Gridiron Battle," *Herald*, 10 October 1909, 9.

26. "Southern Grid Title Still Uncertain," *Herald*, 24 October 1909, 1.

27. "Football," *Kentuckian*, 1911, 131-37; see also Rice, *Wildcats*, 48-49.

28. "State Team Wins From Tennessee by 17-0 Score," *Herald*, 17 October 1909, 1; "Central Eleven Hands Defeat to Transylvania, 32-0," *Herald*, 7 November 1909, 1; "Transylvania Beaten by Louisiana Eleven," *Herald*, 19 November 1909, 6; "Coach Lee Coble Leaves Transylvania," *Herald*, 23 November 1909, 7; "Transylvania Loses to Tennessee Eleven," *Herald*, 26 November 1909, 1.

29. "Thanksgiving Game Will be Spectacular," *Herald*, 24 November 1909, 1; "Championship of State is Won by State University," *Herald*, 26 November 1909, 1.

30. "E.R. Sweetland," *Kentuckian*, 1910, 232; "State University Has Star Eleven, Looks for New Fields to Conquer," *Herald*, 19 November 1909, 4.

31. "Parks May Succeed Sweetland as Coach," *Herald*, 2 November 1909, 6.

32. "Gridiron Rivals Test Team Strength," *Herald*, 12 November 1909, 8; "Football Teams in Pink of Condition," *Herald*, 21 November 1909, 1.

33. "Carolina Athletes are All Heavy Men," *Herald*, 8 October 1910, 3; "State Takes Game of Season," *Herald*, 9 October 1910, 1.

34. "Want Stadium for Stoll Field," *Herald,* 16 November 1910, 3.

35. "Wildcats Visit Enemy's Country," *Herald,* 1 November 1910, 8.

36. "Central Wins State Football Championship," *Herald,* 25 November 1910, 2; "College Reports," *Herald,* 26 November 1910, 4.

37. "Central Says it Will Never Play State Again," *Herald,* 26 November 1910, 1.

38. "Central May Lose Two of Her Best Men," *Herald,* 8 November 1910, 1.

39. "Another Rumpus Among Kentucky Colleges," *Herald,* 16 November 1910, 1; "A Break in Athletics," *Herald,* 20 November 1910, 1.

40. "A Break in Athletics," *Herald,* 20 November 1910, 1.

41. "Sweetland Resigns," *Herald,* 30 November 1910, 1.

42. "Sweetland Resigns," *Idea,* 8 December 1910, 1.

FOUR: A Shelter from the Storm

1. "Football in State University," *Kernel,* 18 November 1915, 4.

2. James Patterson to E.B. Smith, 9 January 1911, James Kennedy Patterson Papers, Special Collections, M.I. King Library North, University of Kentucky, Lexington, Kentucky.

3. BOT Minutes, 31 May 1910, 79; 1 June 1910, 115; 13 December 1910, 121.

4. See Gregory Kent Stanley, "The Flagrant Injustice Done Me By the Board: The Strange and Prolonged Retirement of University of Kentucky President James Kennedy Patterson," *Filson Club History Quarterly* (July 1996).

5. BOT Minutes, 4 June 1913, 17; 5 August 1915, 45.

6. "Football in State University," *Kernel,* 18 November 1915, 4.

7. "Great Rally in Chapel," *Kernel,* 30 November 1911, 1.

8. "Wildcats Beaten by Score of 6-0," *Herald,* 29 October 1911, 1.

9. "Referee Knight Says Let Johnson Play," *Herald,* 3 November 1911, 1.

10. "Transylvania Crimson Tigers Tame Wildcats," *Herald,* 19 November 1911, 4.

11. "A Gridiron Aftermath," *Idea,* 23 November 1911, 7.

12. "Big Expense of Athletic Association," *Idea,* 21 September 1911, 1. There is some doubt as to who was the head coach. A list compiled by the athletic department in 1941 lists Douglass for that spot, while numerous entries in the *Herald,* most notably Webb's testimony in his arson trial, indicate that Webb held the top post.

13. "State in Winning Shows Her Weakness," *Herald,* 1 October 1911, 5; "Morris-Harvey Loses to State University," *Herald,* 8 October 1911, 1; "Wildcats are Beaten by a Score of 6-0," *Herald,* 29 October 1911, 1; "Vandy Beats State in

Hard Fight," *Herald,* 12 November 1911, 1; "Championship Fight Will be a Close One, CU, State and TU Not as Strong as Last Year," *Herald,* 22 October 1911, 3; "Vandy Defeats Central Team, 45-0," *Herald,* 22 October 1911; "Referee Takes Game from Transylvania," *Herald,* 22 October 1911, 4; "Central Defeats Transylvania in a Hard Struggle," *Herald,* 1 December 1911, 1; "Wildcats Win From Tennessee by 12-0 Score," *Herald,* 1 December 1911, 1.

14. "Kentucky Wins from Tennessee," *Idea,* 7 December 1911, 1; "Wildcats Win from Tennessee by 12-0 Score, *Herald,* 1 December 1911, 1.

15. For the period 1911-1938, the UK-UT game was the last of the season for the Wildcats twenty-four times.

16. "Athletic Committee at State Dissolved," *Herald,* 8 May 1912, 1.

17. BOT Minutes, 5 August 1912, 45.

18. "Director of Athletics," *Kentuckian,* 1912, 115; "Assistant Athletic Director, Dick Webb," *Kentuckian,* 1912, 162.

19. "State University to Pull Out of the KIAA," *Herald,* 28 May 1912, 4.

20. "Baseball Victory of State is Knocked Out," *Herald,* 5 June 1912, 4.

21. Ibid.

22. "Park is Suspended From the University Team," *Herald,* 4 January 1913, 3; for a summary of the events, see also, "Thomas Butler Tells Story On Stand in the R.S. Webb Case," *Herald,* 30 April 1913, 1.

23. "Webb is Held to Grand Jury Upon Perjury Charge," *Herald,* 4 January 1913, 1; "Dick Webb on the Witness Stand in His Own Defense," *Herald,* 5 January 1913, 1.

24. "Park is Suspended From the University Team," *Herald,* 31 October 1912, 3. The paper frequently and incorrectly referred to him as Parks.

25. "Office of Anderson Robbed Before Fire," *Herald,* 3 November 1912, 1.

26. BOT Minutes, 10 December 1912, 81-84.

27. "State University Suspended From South's Athletics," *Herald,* 24 November 1912, 1.

28. "State University Triumphant Over Cincinnati Team," *Herald,* 29 November 1912, 1.

29. "Webb is Held to Grand Jury Upon Perjury Charge," *Herald,* 4 January 1913, 1.

30. Ibid., see also, "Dick Webb Chosen Captain of the 1910 Football Eleven at State University," *Leader,* 2 February 1910, 10.

31. Ibid., see also, "Dick Webb on the Witness Stand in His Own Defense," *Herald,* 5 January 1913, 1.

32. "Gerhardt Saw R.S. Webb at Campus on Night of Fire," *Herald,* 10 January 1913, 1.

33. Ibid.

34. Ibid.

35. Ibid.

36. Ibid.; see also, "Webb Trial is to be Resumed this Monday," *Herald*, 6 January 1913, 8.

37. "Webb's Trial Not Completed After All-Day Hearing," *Herald*, 7 January 1913, 1.

38. Ibid.

39. "Richard Webb is Held Over on the Charge of Burning," *Herald*, 11 January 1913, 1.

40. Ibid.; "Webb Indicted on Charge of Burning Anderson's Office," *Herald*, 15 January 1913, 1.

41. "Thomas H. Butler Arrested by Detective Peel at Youngstown," *Herald*, 13 January 1913, 1.

42. "Professor J.J. Tigert New Director for State," *Herald*, 21 January 1913, 3; "Gerhardt Set Free of Perjury Charge by Justice Dodd," *Herald*, 14 January 1913, 1; "Sweetland's Team Wins a Big Big Victory," *Herald*, 28 November 1913, 11.

43. Ibid.

44. Ibid.

45. "Defense Scores on Two Points in the Case Against Webb," *Herald*, 1 May 1913.

46. Ibid.

47. Ibid.

48. Ibid.

49. "Mrs. Webb's Letter Written to Butler is Held Competent," *Herald*, 2 May 1913, 1.

50. "Arguments Finished; Webb Case Goes to the Jury Today," *Herald*, 3 May 1913, 1.

51. Ibid.

52. "Jury Acquits R.S. Webb of the Charge of House Burning," *Herald*, 4 May 1913, 1.

53. "Richard S. Webb Acquitted," *Idea*, 8 May 1913, 1; "Richard S. Webb Declared Innocent of Houseburning," *Leader*, 3 May 1913, 1.

54. BOT Minutes, 4 June 1913, 104-5.

55. Ibid.

56. "Director of Athletics," *Kentuckian*, 1913, 154.

57. "Dozen Men in Practice for Wildcat Battle," *Herald*, 7 September 1913, 5.

58. *Kentuckian*, 1915, 154.

59. BOT Minutes, 29 May 1916; 21 March 1917, 72-75.

60. "Cats Win With Bewildering Passes," *Herald*, 25 October 1914, 1.

61. "City Dump to be State University Athletic Ground," *Leader*, 18 October 1914, 1; "A New Athletic Field," *Idea*, 22 October 1914, 4.

62. "Wildcats Will Start Fall Campaign Today," *Herald*, 9 September 1915, 7.

63. "Blue and White Team has Best Prospects in Years," *Kernel*, 16 September 1915, 1; "Stoll Field to be Dedicated October 8," *Herald*, 17 September 1915, 8; "Wildcats Battle Earlham This Afternoon," *Herald*, 9 October 1915, 8.

64. "Name of Stoll Field Will Still be Used," *Kernel*, 2 October 1915, 5.

65. "University of Kentucky Athletics Endangered by a Lack of Funds," *Leader*, 9 January 1917, 2.

66. Stanley, "Flagrant Injustice."

67. "Wildcats Win in a Spectacular Uphill Battle on Gridiron," *Herald*, 18 October 1914, 1.

68. "Students Got Rough in Their Fun-Making," *Herald*, 26 October 1913, 5; see also Charles Talbert, *The University of Kentucky: The Maturing Years* (Lexington: Univ. of Kentucky Press, 1965), 13.

69. "Wildcats Win in Spectacular Uphill Battle on Gridiron," *Herald*, 18 October 1914, 1; "Earlham-Wildcat Game Today at 2:30," *Herald*, 24 October 1914, 8. Mississippi State was known at that time as Mississippi A&M.

70. "State Almost Ready for Referree's Whistle; Second Week of Practice Has Brought Out the Old Men," *Herald*, 24 September 1911, 1; "High School Team is Beaten by University," *Herald*, 22 October 1911, 3.

71. "Louisville Cancels Game with Wildcats," *Kernel*, 9 November 1916, 1.

72. "Marshall Game Off," *Kernel*, 16 November 1916, 1; "The Football Game Will Not Be Played," *Herald*, 14 November 1913, 9; "Boyd Chambers Tells Why Game Was Cut," *Herald*, 15 November 1913, 7; "Dr. J.J. Tigert Gives His Side of the Case," *Herald*, 16 November 1913, 1.

73. "Dr. Tigert and Coaching Staff," *Kentuckian*, 179; see also "University of Kentucky Head Football Coaches," UK Athletics File, Special Collections, M.I. King Library North, University of Kentucky, Lexington, Kentucky.

FIVE: The Early McVey Years

1. *Kentuckian*, 1924, 131.

2. BOT Minutes, 21 March 1917, 72-73.

3. *Kentuckian*, 1918, 198-99; BOT Minutes, 19 September 1917, 2.

4. *Kentuckian*, 1918, 198.

5. "Florida to Furnish Thanksgiving Meat," *Kernel*, 4 October 1917, 1.

6. "SATC Combined With Camp Buel," *Kernel,* 27 September 1918, 4; "Student Corps Commemorate Founding Today," *Herald,* 1 October 1918, 1; "K.U. Has Trained 800 Men," *Herald,* 4 October 1918, 1. Here the paper refers to the University of Kentucky as KU. "All Day Celebration to be Held October 1," *Kernel,* 27 September 1918, 1.

7. "Athletics Permitted in SATC Colleges," *Kernel,* 27 September 1918, 4. "Big Ten Schedule to Conform to War Department Rules," *Herald,* 9 October 1918, 9; "Gridiron Prospects for Year are Encouraging," *Kernel,* 27 September 1918, 1.

8. "Flu Spreads in Cantonments," *Herald,* 2 October 1918, 1.

9. Alfred W. Crosby, *America's Forgotten Pandemic: The Influenza of 1918* (New York: Cambridge Univ. Press, 1989), 5.

10. Ibid., 11, 25.

11. Ibid., 6-7.

12. Ibid.

13. "No Influenza Among SATC Students," *Kernel,* 4 October 1918, 1; "State Health Board Issues Sweeping Closing Orders in Fight on Spanish Plague," *Herald,* 18 October 1918, 1; "Trots End with Monday's Meet," *Herald,* 9 October 1918, 9.

14. "State Board Issues Sweeping Closing Orders in Fight on Spanish Plague," *Herald,* 18 October 1918, 1; "Influenza Quarantine Bars Town's Students," *Kernel,* 11 October 1918, 1.

15. "First Deaths From Epidemic Reported Here," *Herald,* 9 October 1918, 1.

16. "Flu Situation Still Good in Lexington; Spreads at UK," *Herald,* 3 October 1918, 1; "SATC Enrollment Stopped Until December 20," *Herald,* 9 October 1918, 12; "Many Physical Changes Made on Campus," *Kernel,* 27 September 1918, 1; "Thirteen New Cases of Flu Reported at UK," *Herald,* 16 October 1918, 2.

17. "SATC Men Must Finish Their Courses," *Herald,* 22 October 1918, 8; "Health Chiefs Opposed to University Opening," *Herald,* 2 November 1918, 3.

18. "Flu Well in Hand," *Kernel,* 11 November 1918, 7; "No Game Thanksgiving," *Herald,* 27 November 1918, 1.

19. BOT Minutes, 10 December 1918, 92; "Flu Well In Hand," *Kernel,* 11 November 1918, 7.

20. "2,000 Flu Cases in Breathitt County," *Herald,* 25 October 1918, 2; "Flu Ban Still on in Lexington," *Herald,* 20 November 1918, 10.

21. Crosby, *America's Forgotten Pandemic,* 64.

22. Judy Gail Cornett, "Angel for the Blind: The Public Triumphs and Private Tragedies of Linda Neville" (Ph.D. diss., University of Kentucky, 1993).

23. Crosby, *America's Forgotten Pandemic,* 208-15.

24. "Reconstruction at KU Arrives with Armistice; Students Will be Classified Under Old Schedule," *Herald*, 15 November 1918, 6; see also Talbert, *University of Kentucky*, 50-51.

25. "Student Army Corps at KU is Ordered Demobilized," *Herald*, 28 November 1918, 10; "Goodbye Barracks, Exit Camp Buell," *Kernel*, 6 January 1919, 2; *Kentuckian*, 1919, 146.

26. *Kentuckian*, 1922, 130-31.

27. "Price McLean Dies Following Injury in Game," *Herald*, 8 October 1923, 1; "Price McLean, Varsity Center, Dies of Injury Received During Game," *Kernel*, 12 October 1923, 1.

28. "Price McLean Dies Following Injury in Game," *Herald*, 8 October 1923, 1. For accounts of fatalities at other schools mentioned in the *Herald*, see, "Cadet's Death May End Army Football," 1 November 1909, 1; "Football Player Held Not Guilty," 15 November 1910, 6; "Nineteen Football Fatalities So Far," 23 November 1910, 5; "Gridiron Hero is Dying," 25 October 1909, 3.

29. "To Hold McLean Funeral Today," *Herald*, 9 October 1923, 1.

30. "Memorial Services for Price McLean," *Kernel*, 12 October 1923, 1.

31. "Wildcat Football Squad Suspends Practice Today and Will Pay Last Respects at Fallen Comrade's Bier," *Herald*, 9 October 1923, 7; "Game Rally in Last Period Gives Wildcats 6 to 6 Tie with Washington and Lee," *Herald*, 14 October 1923, 1.

32. "Rush Plans in Building Football Stadium for Completion," September 1924, *Kernel*, 12 October 1923, 1.

33. "If Other Colleges Did, So Can Kentucky," *Kernel*, 13 April 1923, 1.

34. "Students and Faculty Oversubscribe Quota in New Stadium Drive," *Kernel*, 23 April 1923, 1.

35. "Captain Calhoun to Lead $200,000 Campaign of U of K," *Kernel*, 18 May 1923, 1.

36. "The Story of the University of Kentucky Stadium," pamphlet dated March 1925, in University of Kentucky Buildings File, McLean Stadium Folder, Special Collection, M.I. King Library North, University of Kentucky, Lexington, Kentucky.

37. BOT Minutes, 7 April 1924, 209; "Three Sites are to be Viewed in Location of New Football Stadium," *Kernel*, 29 November 1923, 1.

38. BOT Minutes, 7 April 1924, 209; "Stadium Site Fixed at Southwest Corner of Rose and Winslow Streets," *Kernel*, 11 April 1924, 1. The southwest corner of Rose and Winslow Streets was along the eastern edge of Stoll Field.

39. BOT Minutes, 2 May 1924, 229; "Stadium Contract Awarded to Louis des Cognets for $100,000," *Kernel*, 2 May 1924, 1.

40. "Stadium Site Fixed at Southwest Corner of Rose and Winslow Streets," *Kernel,* 11 April 1924, 1; "Stadium Contract Awarded to Louis des Cognets for $100,000," *Kernel,* 2 May 1924, 1.

41. BOT Minutes, 9 December 1924, 287-89.

42. "Stadium Is to Be Ready for Game With Louisville," *Kernel,* 26 September 1924, 1; "Kentucky Line Has Strength," *Herald,* 5 October 1924, 6; "Generals Beat Cats, 10-7," *Herald,* 19 October 1924, 1.

43. "Plan Exercises at UK Stadium," *Herald,* 9 October 1924, 1.

44. "Stadium Will Be Dedicated Stoll Field Between Halves of Game Saturday," *Herald,* 30 October 1924, 16; "Colonels Conquer Wildcats, 7-0," *Herald,* 2 November 1924, 1.

45. "Story of the University of Kentucky Stadium," 20.

SIX: Banning Women's Sports

1. Sarah Blanding to F.B. Lambert, 13 December 1923, Dean of Women Papers, Physical Education File, Special Collections, M.I. King Library North, University of Kentucky, Lexington, Kentucky.

2. Sophia Foster Richardson, "Tendencies in Athletics for Women in Colleges and Universities," *Popular Science,* February 1897, 517-18.

3. Edward H. Clarke, *Sex in Education; or a Fair Chance for the Girls* (1873, rpt., Arno), 1972.

4. BOT Minutes, 5 June 1900, 23; 10 December 1901, 61-62.

5. Mary Elizabeth Payne, "Florence Offutt Stout, Teacher of Physical Education at the University of Kentucky for Forty Years" (M.A. thesis, University of Kentucky, 1941).

6. BOT Minutes, 10 December 1901, 79-85; see also, 12 December 1900, 23.

7. BOT Minutes, 3 June 1902, 112. Stout was promoted to full professor status during the 1906-1907 academic year; see also, Payne, "Florence Offutt Stout," 7.

8. Lucy Blackburn to Board of Trustees, 7 December 1903, recorded in BOT Minutes, 9 December 1903, 241.

9. Ibid.

10. Ibid., 243.

11. BOT Minutes, 28 September 1912, 54; 26 October 1912, 56; 10 December 1912, 65.

12. For a fuller account of nineteenth-century gymnastic drill, see Gregory Kent Stanley, *The Rise and Fall of the Sportswoman: Women's Health, Fitness, and Athletics, 1860-1940* (New York: Peter Lang, 1996).

13. Hopkins, *University of Kentucky,* 169.

14. Minutes of the Faculty, 12 November 1909, 560. Special Collections, M.I. King Library North, University of Kentucky, Lexington, Kentucky.

15. Minutes of the Executive Committee, 13 November 1909, 2, Special Collections, M.I. King Library North, University of Kentucky, Lexington, Kentucky.

16. Minutes of the Executive Committee, 8 November 1910.

17. Minutes of the Faculty, 14 January 1910.

18. Minutes of the Faculty, 10 February 1910, 567-68.

19. Minutes of the Faculty, 4 March 1910.

20. Ibid.

21. Minutes of the Faculty, 12 April 1910.

22. Ibid.

23. Minutes of the Executive Committee, 23 August 1910, 378.

24. BOT Minutes, 3 June 1911, 261; 25 July 1912, 203; 5 August 1913, 45.

25. The lessons were discontinued in 1916, but the issue was not resolved until 1920. Under the agreement reached with Stout, the trustees, and new president McVey, Stout had to reimburse the university for its expenses (coal, electricity, and pool maintenance); see BOT Minutes, 26 April 1920, 11.

26. See copies of the *Kentuckian* from 1910 to 1925.

27. Florence Stout to Frank McVey, 18 February 1918, Frank L. McVey Papers, Box 14, Department of Physical Education for Women File; "Report of 1918 Physical Examination," McVey Papers, Box 14, Department of Physical Education for Women File, Special Collections, M.I. King Library North, University of Kentucky, Lexington, Kentucky.

28. Josephine Simrall and Florence Stout to Frank McVey, 17 March 1920, McVey Papers, Box 14.

29. Frank McVey to Josephine Simrall, 24 March 1920, Dean of Women Papers, Physical Education File.

30. Frank McVey to Florence Stout, 9 November 1923, McVey Papers, Box 14.

31. Florence Stout to Frank McVey, 11 December 1923, McVey Papers, Box 14.

32. BOT Minutes, 6 June 1919, 96; 20 July 1923, 79. In 1926 she transferred from physical education to political science, BOT Minutes, 29 May 1926, 12.

33. "Girls Not to Play," *Herald,* 19 September 1924, 10.

34. "Girls' Basketball to be Abolished, Former Team Members Request Senate to Reconsider," *Kernel,* 3 October 1924, 1.

35. "Girls Not to Play," *Herald,* 19 September 1924, 10.

36. Cited in Frank McVey to Florence Stout, 9 November 1923, McVey Papers, Box 14, Department of Physical Education for Women File.

37. "Student Forum: Why Has Girls' Intercollegiate Basketball Been Banned?" *Kernel*, 3 October 1924, 4.

38. "Girls to Appeal Council Action," *Kernel*, 24 October 1924, 1.

39. Ibid.

40. "Women's Athletic Association Abolishes Intercollegiate Sport for Girls," *Kernel*, 21 November 1924.

41. See, Stephen St. Clair, "The Play Day/Sports Day Movement in Selected Colleges" (Ed.D. thesis, University of North Carolina, 1984); Mabel Lee, *A History of Physical Education and Sports in the USA* (New York: John Wiley and Sons, 1983).

42. "Sport Renewed for UK Coeds," *Kernel*, 24 November 1933, 1.

43. Sarah Blanding to Frank McVey, 27 December 1928, McVey Papers, Box 14.

44. See the student yearbooks for the period 1925-1930.

45. Ellen Gerber, "The Controlled Development of Collegiate Sports for Women," *Journal of Sport History* (Spring 1975): 6-7.

46. BOT Minutes, 31 May 1924, 229.

47. "New Girls' Gym is Open Today, Old Boys' Gym is Converted During the Summer," *Kernel*, 3 October 1924, 1.

48. Florence Stout to Frank McVey, 17 March 1920, McVey Papers, Box 14.

49. Lee, *History of Physical Education,* 162-63; See also, Alice Sefton, *The Women's Division, National Amateur Athletic Federation; Sixteen Years of Progress in Athletics for Girls and Women* (Stanford: Stanford Univ. Press, 1941).

50. "National Platform," Women's Division, National Amateur Athletic Federation, in Dean of Women Papers, Physical Education File, University of Kentucky. See also, Lee, *History of Physical Education,* 158-63; St. Clair, "Play Day/ Sport Day Movement," 24.

51. "Athletic Strenuosity," *American Physical Education Review* (July 1925): 54.

52. Helen Coops, "Sports for Women," *American Physical Education Review* (November 1926): 1088.

53. "National Platform, NAAF," in Dean of Women Papers; see also Lee, *History of Physical Education,* 158.

54. F.B. Lambert to Sarah Blanding, 6 December 1923; Sarah Blanding to F.B. Lambert, 13 December 1923, Dean of Women Papers, Physical Education File.

55. "Louisville Basketball Qunitet Will Meet Lexington Outfit Here Tonight," *Herald,* 16 February 1923, 8; see also, "Impressive Victory is Scored by Kittenettes: Too Much Blanding," *Herald,* 23 February 1923, 1.

56. Anna Norris to Sarah Blanding, no date, Dean of Women Papers; see also Norris cited in Mabel Lee, "A Consideration of the Fundamental Differences Between Boys and Girls as They Affect the Girls' Program of Physical Education," *Education* (April 1933): 468.

SEVEN: From Humble Origins to Signature Sport

1. "Basketball," *Kentuckian*, 1939, 108.

2. Bert Nelli, *The Winning Tradition: A History of Kentucky Wildcat Basketball* (Lexington: Univ. Press of Kentucky, 1988).

3. Ibid.

4. Cone, *University of Kentucky*, 34.

5. "Review of the Basket Ball Season," *Kentuckian*, 1909, 181-83.

6. "Stop Basketball at State University," *Herald*, 20 November 1909, 3.

7. "Basket Ball," *Idea*, 25 November 1909, 2; "A Coach for Basket and Base Ball," *Idea*, 2 December 1909, 8.

8. "Basket Ball," *Idea*, 25 November 1909, 2; "Basket Ball," *Idea*, 9 December 1909, 1; "Basket Ball," *Idea*, January 1910, 1; BOT Minutes, 7 December 1909.

9. "Basketball," *Kentuckian*, 1910.

10. "Review of Season," *Kentuckian*, 1912, 139.

11. "Professor J.J. Tigert New Director for State," *Herald*, 21 January 1913, 3.

12. The student yearbook employed the "Bucheit" spelling.

13. "Dr. Tigert and Coaching Staff," *Kentuckian*, 1917, 179.

14. "Cats Leave for SIAA Today," *Herald*, 24 February 1921, 5.

15. "Kentucky Five Wins Southern Basketball Championship in Thrilling Contest," *Herald*, 2 March 1921, 5; see also, "UK Defeats Georgia Bulldog," *Kentuckian*, 1922, 140. The 1921 yearbook had gone to press before the 1921 championship game. Coverage of the contest provided the lead story for the 1922 yearbook basketball section.

16. "Rooters Watch Wildcats Win, Follow Game by Telegraph," *Herald*, 2 May 1921, 5.

17. "University Takes Holiday to Do Honor to its Conquering Heroes," *Herald*, 3 May 1921, 7.

18. "At the End of the First Half of the 1922 Basketball Season," *Kentuckian*, 1922, 141-42.

19. Nelli, *Winning Tradition*, 22.

20. BOT Minutes, 26 January 1923, 12-13.

21. BOT Minutes, 12 June 1923, 63.

22. BOT Minutes, 26 January 1923, 6-7.

23. BOT Minutes, 23 March 1923, 8-9.

24. BOT Minutes, 20 July 1923, 76.

25. BOT Minutes, 2 October 1923, 101; 15 October 1912, 114-16.

26. BOT Minutes, 15 October 1923, 114-16; 19 December 1923, 158-69.

27. Report of the Business Agent, in BOT Minutes, 19 October 1923, 143; BOT Minutes, 9 December 1923, 158-69.

28. Ibid.; see also, BOT Minutes, 4 April 1924, 202-6.

29. BOT Minutes, 31 May 1924, 228-29; 2 July 1924, 6-8; 9 December 1924, 286.

30. "Basketball, 1924-1925," *Kentuckian,* 1925, 103.

31. "Kitten Football Team," *Kentuckian,* 1926, 97.

32. "Basketball Season of 1926," *Kentuckian,* 1926, 102-4.

33. BOT Minutes, 14 December 1926, 15.

34. "Hayden to Coach Wildcat Basketball," *Herald,* 1 December 1926, 12.

35. Ibid.; see also BOT Minutes, 16 February 1924, 188.

36. "Basketball," *Kentuckian,* 1927, 85-87; "Wildcats Open Conference Season Tonight," *Herald,* 3 January 1927, 6; "Panthers Beat State, 31-24," *Herald,* 11 January 1927, 6.

37. "Varsity Basketball," *Kentuckian,* 128, 220.

38. "Varsity Basketball," *Kentuckian,* 1930, 274.

39. "Varsity Basketball," *Kentuckian,* 1929, 236-37.

40. Nelli, *Winning Tradition,* 34.

41. BOT Minutes, 31 May 1930, 25; 16 July 1929, 9; 7 February 1929, 2.

42. Nelli, *Winning Tradition,* 37.

43. "Kansan Accepts Two-Year Offer to Coach Cats," *Kernel,* 23 May 1930.

44. Dan Chandler and Vernon Hatton, *Rupp from Both Ends of the Bench* (Published by the authors, 1972); Harry Lancaster, *Adolph Rupp as I Knew Him* (Lexington: Lexington Productions, 1979).

45. "Varsity Basketball," *Kentuckian,* 1931, 222.

46. Joe Creason, "Basketball," *Kentuckian,* 1939, 108.

47. Cone, *University of Kentucky;* see also Talbert, *University of Kentucky.*

48. "Varsity Basketball," *Kentuckian,* 1935, 110.

49. "Basketball," *Kentuckian,* 1938, 100-101.

50. BOT Minutes, 13 March 1936, 53; 6 April 1937, 22-23.

EIGHT: Expansion, Depression, and Fiscal Chaos

1. BOT Minutes, 26 April 1920, 12; 26 January 1923, 13; 16 February 1924, 188; 27 February 1929, 2; 17 January 1934, 20. Athletic department financial statements did not account for these subsidies.

2. "Wildcats to Hold Spring Practice," *Kernel,* 7 December 1920, 1.

3. "Cat Gridders to Have New Mentor for 1924," *Kernel,* 18 January 1924, 6.

4. BOT Minutes, 16 February 1924, 188.

5. F.C. Forbs to Frank McVey, 29 December 1924, reprinted in BOT Minutes, 13 January 1926, 8-9.

6. F.C. Forbs to Frank McVey, 4 January 1926, reprinted in BOT Minutes, 13 January 1926, 8-9.

7. BOT Minutes, 23 June 1926, 10.

8. BOT Minutes, 2 February 1927, 1-3; J.P. Johnston to Frank McVey, 11 February 1927, reprinted in BOT Minutes, 16 March 1927, 6.

9. BOT Minutes, 23 September 1930, 14-15.

10. Report of the Athletic Association Audit, BOT Minutes, 24 February 1931, 9-12.

11. Ibid.

12. Talbert, *University of Kentucky,* 95-96.

13. BOT Minutes, 9 March 1932, 13-14.

14. BOT Minutes, 18 April 1932, 12-13.

15. BOT Minutes, 13 July 1932, 6.

16. BOT Minutes, 4 June 1932, 7.

17. BOT Minutes, 29 April 1932, 5.

18. BOT Minutes, 13 December 1932, 5-7.

19. "Gamage's Success Predicted by Zuppke," *Herald,* 23 January 1927, 5.

20. "Varsity Football," *Kentuckian,* 1931, 209.

21. BOT Minutes, 1 June 1933, 7.

22. BOT Minutes, 12 November, 1933, 5; see also Talbert, *University of Kentucky,* 114.

23. "Harry Gamage Resigns as Head Football Coach," *Kernel,* 24 November 1933, 1.

24. "Wynne is Selected by Council," *Kernel,* 8 December 1933, 1; "Wynne Will be UK Coach," *Kernel,* 15 December 1933, 1; "Football Coach," *Kernel,* 14 September 1934, 1.

25. BOT Minutes, 17 January 1934, 20.

26. BOT Minutes, 15 December 1931, 6; 23 July 1936, 6.

27. BOT Minutes, 23 September 1936, 9-10.

28. "Wildcat Games to Be Broadcast Through WHAS," *Kernel,* 29 September 1936, 1.

29. BOT Minutes, 23 September 1936, 15.

30. BOT Minutes, 14 October 1936, 26.

31. BOT Minutes, 31 October 1935, 19-20; 23 July 1936, 7-10.

32. BOT Minutes, 8 December 1936, 4.

NINE: The Purge of 1938

1. "Memo: In Re: Wynne," undated memo signed by Frank L. McVey, Frank L. McVey Papers, Box 75, Folder 2, Athletic Controversy File. Special Collections, M.I. King Library North, University of Kentucky, Lexington, Kentucky.

2. Ibid.

3. "The Bull Pen," *Kernel,* 17 September 1937, 1-2.

4. "Jackets Repeat '36 Rout; Skin Cats 52-0," *Kernel,* 12 October 1937, 1; "Stoll's Top Mob Watches Tennessee Beat Kentucky," *Kernel,* 11 November 1937, 1; "Bull Pen," *Kernel,* 30 November 1937, 1; "Sub's 58-Yard Dash Jockies Florida into 6-0 Triumph," *Kernel,* 7 December 1937, 1; "Bull Pen," *Kernel,* 7 December 1937, 4.

5. "Sub's 58-Yard Dash Jockies Florida Into 6-0 Triumph Over Kentucky as Vacant Pews See Curtain Clash," *Kernel,* 7 December 1937, 1; see also, Neville Dunn, "Top O' the Morning," *Herald,* 7 January 1938, 8.

6. BOT Minutes, 24 February 1938, 40-42; Neville Dunn, "Top O' the Morning," *Herald,* 7 January 1938, 8; "Alumni Group Asks Dismissal of Coach Wynne," *Herald,* 12 February 1938, 1.

7. "Squad Threatens En Masse Quit Unless Try is Made to Reobtain Aids," *Kernel,* 11 January 1938, 1; "70 Football Players Demand Reinstatement of Two Assistant Coaches," *Herald,* 11 January 1938, 1.

8. "Tom Gorman, Line Coach, Joins Football Abdicators," *Kernel,* 7 January 1938, 4; "70 Football Players Demand Reinstatement of Two Assistant Coaches," *Herald,* 11 January 1938, 1.

9. Ibid.

10. "Reorganization of UK Athletic Department in Resolution by Council," *Herald,* 14 January 1938, 1.

11. "Investigation of Athletic Department of UK May Continue Three or Four Weeks," *Herald,* 16 January 1938, 26.

12. "Members of Football Team Reverses Plan; Would Restrict Alumni Representation," *Herald,* 19 January 1938, 1.

13. Ibid.; see also, "UK Gridders to Repudiate Committee Plan," *Herald,* 21 January 1938, 1.

14. "Football," *Herald,* 26 November 1896, 5; "The Football Game," *Herald,* 3 October 1896, 12; "LAC Defeated," *Herald,* 27 November 1896, 1. Muir coached for a brief period at Presbyterian University in Clarksville, Tennessee.

15. "Members of UK Football Team Reverse Plan: Would Restrict Alumni Representatives," *Herald,* 19 January 1938, 1.

16. Ibid.; see also, Wallace Muir to M.E. Ligon, 17 January 1938, Frank L. McVey Papers, Box 75, Folder 2, Athletic Controversy File.

17. "Members of Football Team Reverse Plan: Would Restrict Alumni Representation," *Herald,* 19 January 1938, 1; "Editorial: Football at the University," *Herald,* 21 January 1938, 4.

18. "Urge Removal of Chet Wynne," *Herald,* 30 January 1938, 18.

19. "Alumni Group asks Dismissal of Coach Wynne," *Herald,* 12 February 1938, 1; "No Announcement Made by UK Committee," *Herald,* 13 February 1938, 24.

20. M.E. Potter, to Frank McVey, 19 February 1938, McVey Papers, Box 75, Folder 2, Athletic Controversy File.

21. M.E. Potter to P.P. Boyd, 29 January 1938, McVey Papers, Box 75, Folder 2, Athletic Controversy File.

22. "Muir and Boles," undated memo, McVey Papers, Box 75, Folder 2, Athletic Controversy File.

23. "Coaches," "Players," undated memos, McVey Papers, Box 75, Folder 2, Athletic Controversy File.

24. "Resignation of Chet Wynne as UK Athletic Director and Football Coach Reported," *Herald,* 18 February 1938, 1.

25. "Chet Wynne Resigns as UK Athletic Director and Football Coach," *Herald,* 19 February 1938, 1.

26. Ibid.

27. Marvin Gay, "Gay-zing at Sports," *Kernel,* 25 February 1938, 1; "Executive Board Gives Nod to Shively, Kirwan, Athletic Reformation Plan Approved," *Kernel,* 25 February 1938, 1; BOT Minutes, 24 February 1938, 40-42.

28. "Athletic Director Committee to Report to Dr. McVey Tuesday," *Herald,* 20 February 1938, 24; "Bernie Shively is Recommended as University Athletic Director," *Herald,* 22 February 1938, 1; "Shively is Group's Choice," *Kernel,* 22 February 1938, 1; see also, Rice, *Wildcats,* 348.

29. BOT Minutes, 24 February 1938, 40-42.

30. "Bernie Shively and Ab Kirwan Work While They Eat," *Herald,* 22 February 1938, 5; "Shively Boosts Booster Clubs to Kentucky Alumni," *Kernel,* 12 April 1938, 1; "Booster Clubs Plan Meetings," *Kernel,* 26 April 1938, 1.

31. "Football," *Kentuckian,* 1939, 101-5.

32. *Kentuckian,* 1940, 116-20.

EPILOGUE

1. Talbert, *University of Kentucky,* 100.

2. Ibid., 164-65.

3. BOT Minutes, 7 June 1940, 8; 2 April 1940, 10.
4. "Stadium Plans are Condensed," *Herald,* 4 May 1948, 8.
5. "Goodbye McLean Stadium," *Herald,* 16 August 1974, 4.
6. Rupp Arena is not actually on campus but rather in downtown Lexington.

◻

BIBLIOGRAPHY

UNIVERSITY OF KENTUCKY
ARCHIVAL MATERIALS

Athletics File
Henry S. Barker Papers
Sarah Blanding Papers
Buildings File
Dean of Women Papers
Frank L. McVey Papers
Minutes of the Board of Trustees
Minutes of the Executive Committee
Minutes of the Faculty
James K. Patterson Papers
Richard C. Stoll Biographical File
Student Newspapers: *Idea, Kernel*
Student Yearbooks: *Memoria, Echoes, Kentuckian*

LEXINGTON NEWSPAPERS

Lexington *Herald* (listed as *Morning Herald* in the late nineteenth century)
Lexington *Leader*

UNIVERSITY-RELATED PUBLICATIONS

Chandler, Dan, and Vernon Hatton. *Rupp From Both Ends of the Bench.* Published by the authors, 1972.

Cone, Carl. *The University of Kentucky: A Pictorial History.* Lexington: Univ. Press of Kentucky, 1988.

Hopkins, James F. *The University of Kentucky: Origins and Early Years.* Lexington: Univ. of Kentucky Press, 1951.

Irvin, Helen Deiss. *Hail Kentucky! A Pictorial History of the University of Kentucky.* Lexington: Univ. of Kentucky Press, 1965.

Lancaster, Harry. *Adolph Rupp as I Knew Him.* Lexington: Lexington Productions, 1979.

Nelli, Bert. *The Winning Tradition: A History of Kentucky Wildcat Basketball.* Lexington: Univ. Press of Kentucky, 1984.

Pollitt, Mabel. *A Biography of James Kennedy Patterson, President of the University of Kentucky from 1869-1910.* Louisville: Westerfield-Bonte, 1925.

Rice, Russell. *The Wildcats: A Story of Kentucky Football.* Huntsville, Ala: Strode Publishers, 1975.

Stanley, Gregory Kent. "The Flagrant Injustice Done Me by the Board: The Strange and Prolonged Retirement of University of Kentucky President James Kennedy Patterson." *Filson Club History Quarterly* (July 1996).

Talbert, Charles G. *The University of Kentucky: The Maturing Years.* Lexington: Univ. of Kentucky Press, 1965.

MISCELLANEOUS SOURCES

"Athletic Strenuosity." *American Physical Education Review* (July 1925).

Beard, George. *American Nervousness: Its Causes and Consequences.* 1881; rpt., New York: Arno, 1972.

Castle, William. *Heredity and Eugenics.* Chicago: Univ. of Chicago Press, 1912.

Coops, Helen. "Sports for Women." *American Physical Education Review* (November 1926).

Cornett, Judy Gail. "Angel for the Blind: The Public Triumphs and Private Tragedies of Linda Neville." Ph.D. diss., University of Kentucky, 1993.

Crosby, Alfred W. *America's Forgotten Pandemic: The Influenza of 1918.* New York: Cambridge Univ. Press, 1989.

Gerber, Ellen. "The Controlled Development of Collegiate Sports for Women." *Journal of Sport History* (Spring 1975).

Lee, Mabel. "A Consideration of the Fundamental Differences Between Boys and Girls as They Affect the Girls' Program of Physical Education." *Education* (April 1933).

———. *A History of Physical Education and Sport in the USA.* New York: John Wiley and Sons, 1983.

Payne, Mary Elizabeth. "Florence Offutt Stout, Teacher of Physical Education at the University of Kentucky for Forty Years." M.A. thesis, University of Kentucky, 1941.

Ripley, William Z. *The Races of Europe: A Sociological Study.* New York: Appleton, 1899.

Roosevelt, Theodore. "The Law of Civilization and Decay." *Forum* (January 1897).

Sefton, Alice. *The Women's Division, National Amateur Athletic Federation: Sixteen Years of Progress in Athletics for Girls and Women.* Stanford: Stanford University Press, 1941.

Smith, Ronald A. *Sports and Freedom: The Rise of Big-Time College Athletics.* New York: Oxford Univ. Press, 1988.

Stanley, Gregory Kent. *The Rise and Fall of the Sportswoman: Women's Health, Fitness, and Athletics, 1860-1940.* New York: Peter Lang, 1996.

St. Clair, Stephen. "The Play Day/Sports Day Movement in Selected Colleges." Ed.D. thesis, University of North Carolina at Greensboro, 1984.

INDEX